THE
Christian Christmas
SONGBOOK

Christian
Christmas
songbook
Christian
Christmas
Songbook
Christian
Christmas
Songbook

ISBN 0-634-04760-4

HAL•LEONARD®
CORPORATION

7777 W. BLUEMOUND RD. P.O. BOX 13819 MILWAUKEE, WI 53213

Visit Hal Leonard Online at
www.halleonard.com

CONTENTS

ALL IS WELL

Words and Music by MICHAEL W. SMITH
and WAYNE KIRKPATRICK

Meditative ♩ = 76

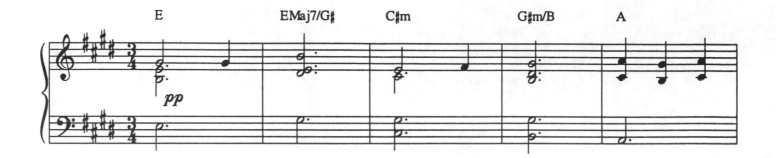

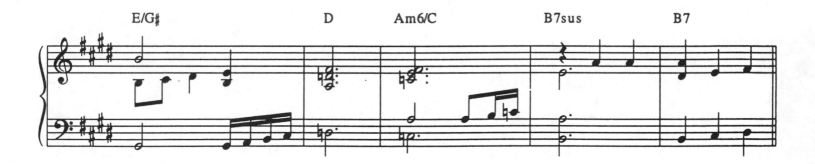

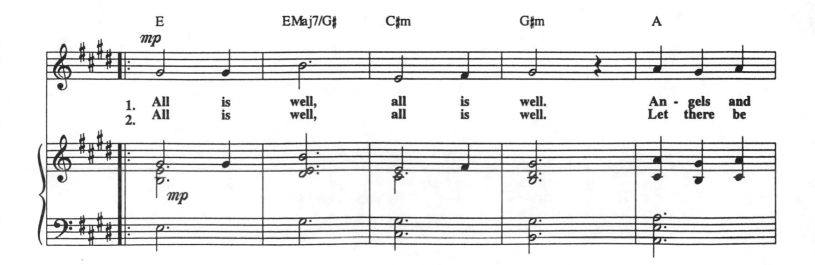

1. All is well, all is well. An - gels and
2. All is well, all is well. Let there be

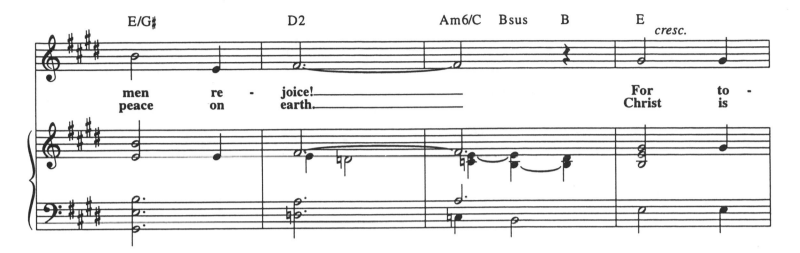

men re - joice!_____ For to -
peace on earth._____ Christ is

night_____ dark - ness fell in - to the
come,_____ go and tell that He is

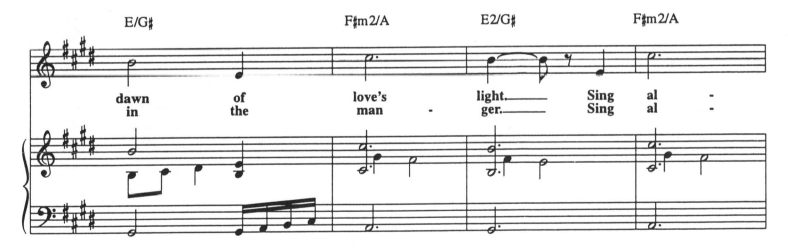

dawn of love's light._____ Sing al -
in of the man - ger._____ Sing al -

le,_____ sing al - le - lu - ia!_____
le,_____ sing al - le - lu - ia!_____

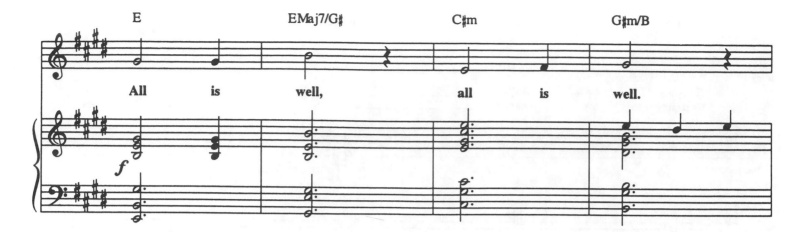

All is well, all is well.

Lift up your voice and sing.___

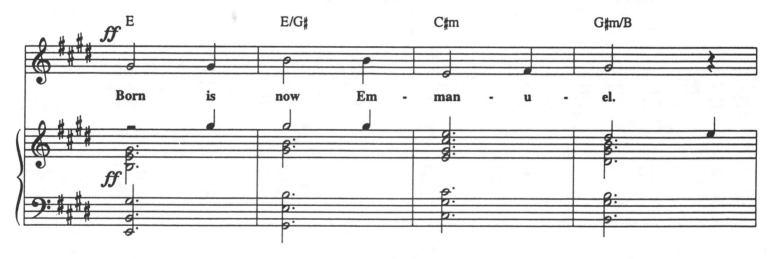

Born is now Em - man - u - el.

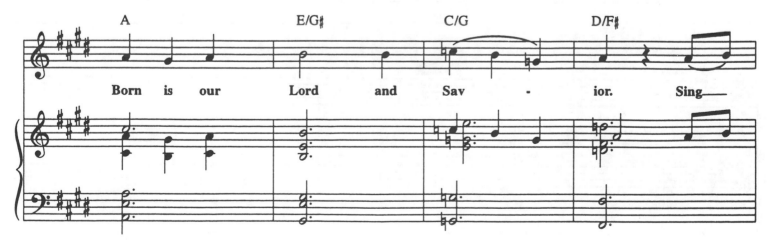

Born is our Lord and Sav - ior. Sing___

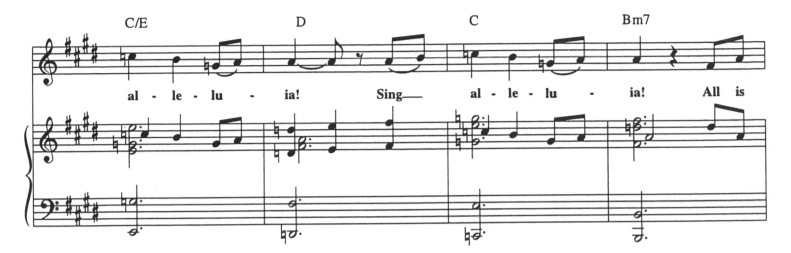

al - le - lu - ia! Sing____ al - le - lu - ia! All is

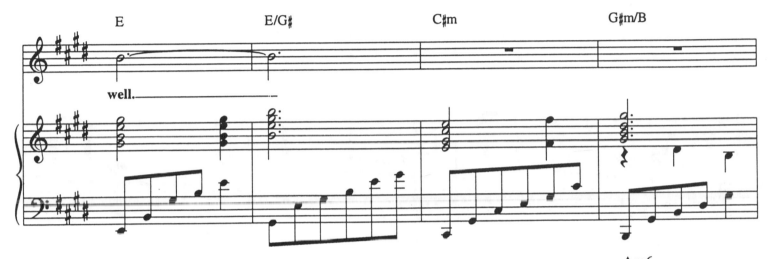

well._____

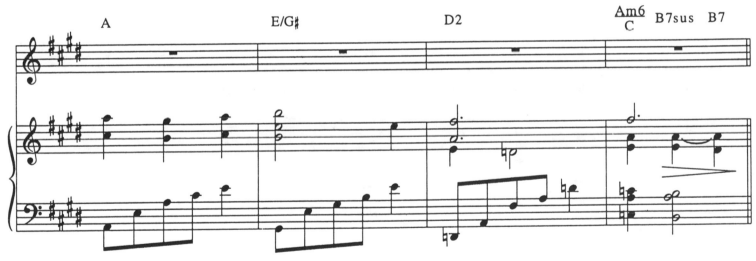

Born   is   now   Em - man - u - el.

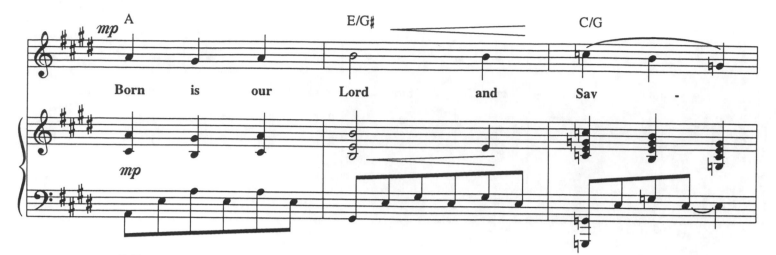

Born is our Lord and Sav -

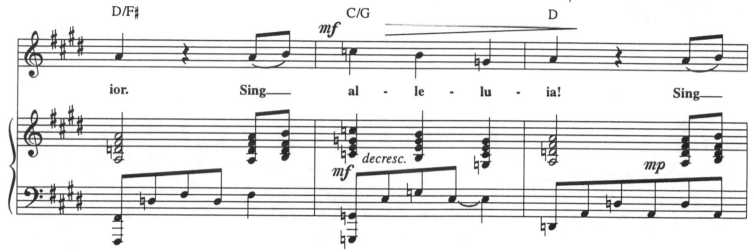

ior. Sing___ al - le - lu - ia! Sing___

al - le - lu - ia! All is well.___

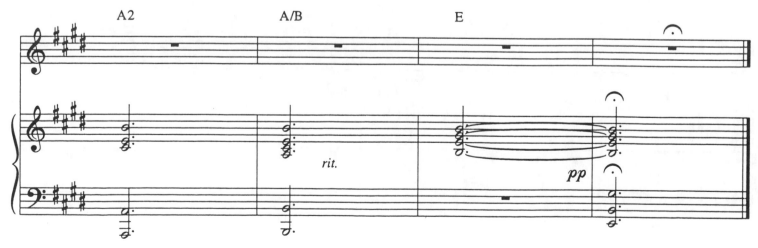

ALL MY HEART REJOICES

Words and Music by
STEVE GREEN

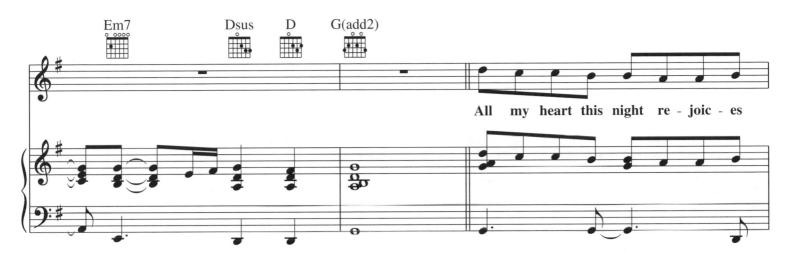

All my heart this night re-joic-es

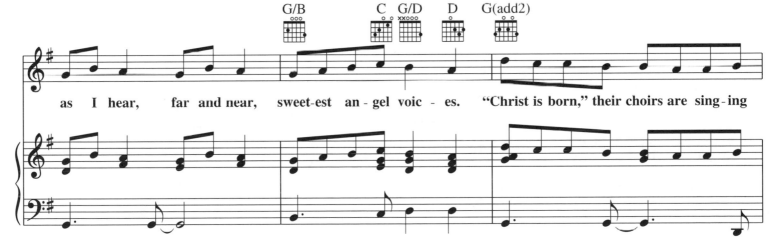

as I hear, far and near, sweet-est an-gel voic-es. "Christ is born," their choirs are sing-ing

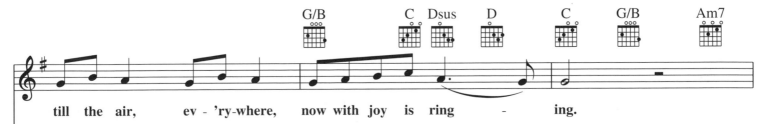

till the air, ev-'ry-where, now with joy is ring - ing.

of the Lord. __ All my heart re - joice to - night.

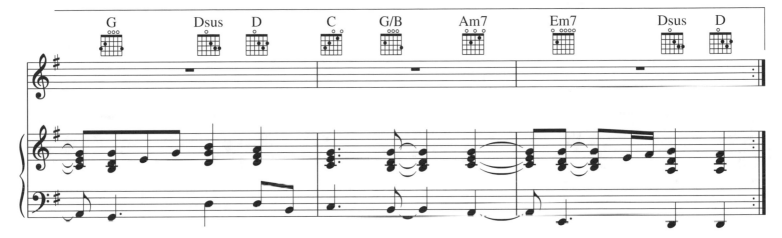

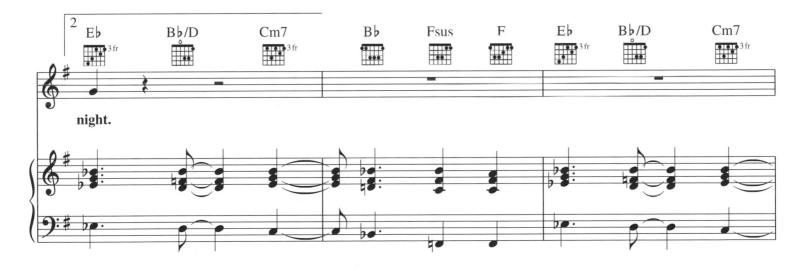

night.

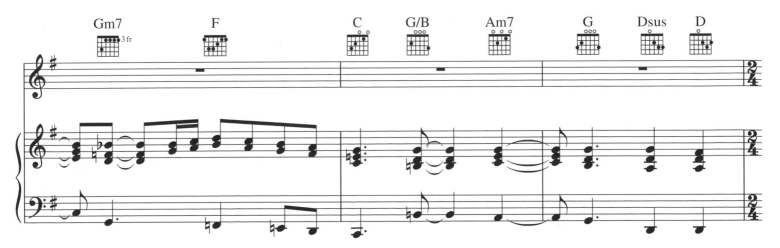

ANGELS WE HAVE HEARD ON HIGH

Words by EDWARD BARNES
Music by STEVEN CURTIS CHAPMAN

In a steady four

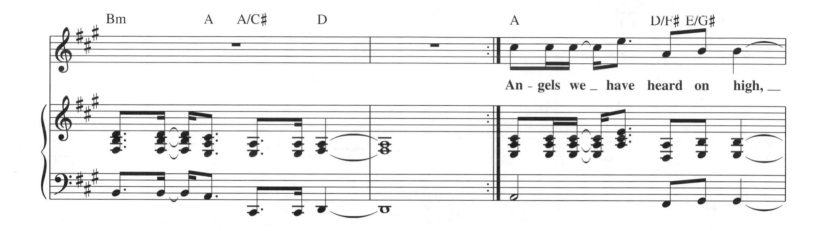

An - gels we _ have heard on high, _

sweet - ly sing - ing o'er the plains, _

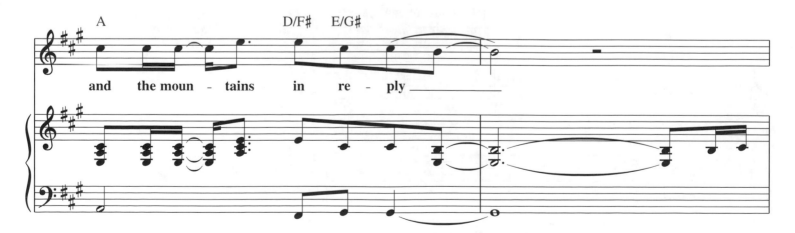

and the moun - tains in re - ply _

15

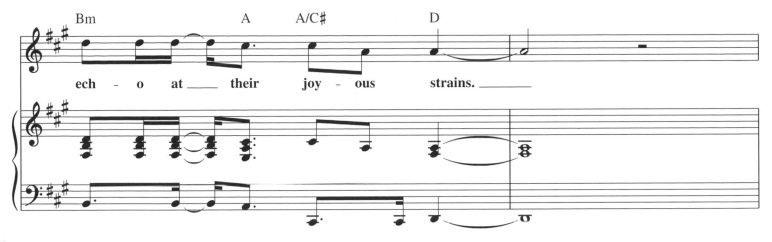

ech - o at their joy - ous strains.

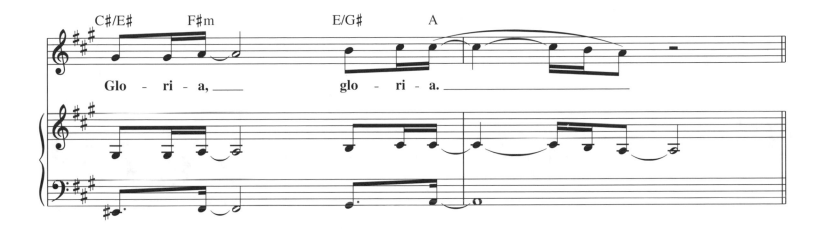

Glo - ri - a, gloria.

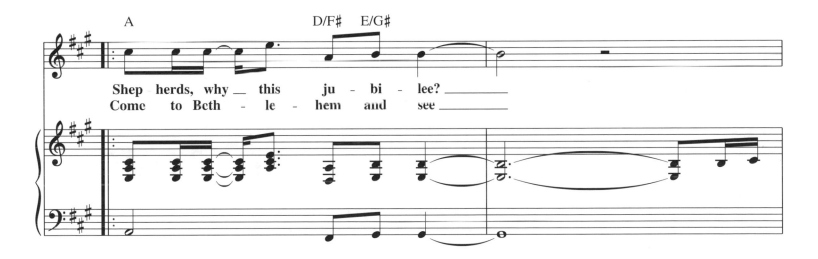

Shep - herds, why this ju - bi - lee?
Come to Beth - le - hem and see

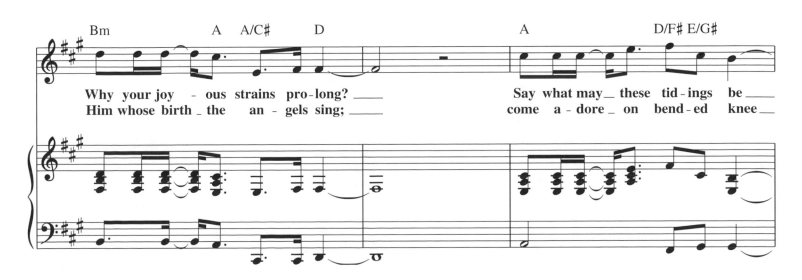

Why your joy - ous strains pro - long?
Him whose birth the an - gels sing;

Say what may these tid - ings be
come a - dore on bend - ed knee

which in - spire _ your heav - en - ly song? _
Christ, the Lord, _ the new - born King. _

Glo - ri - a, _ glo - ri - a. _

Glo. . .

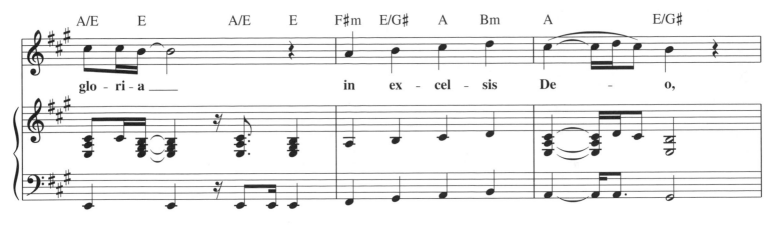

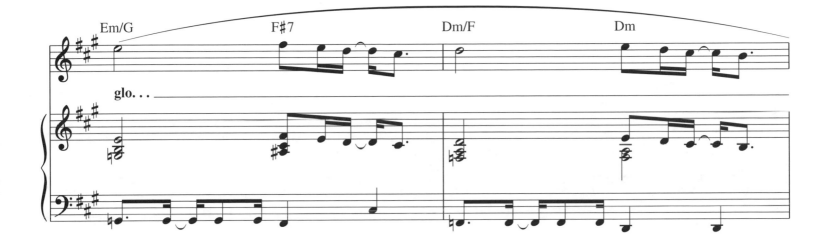

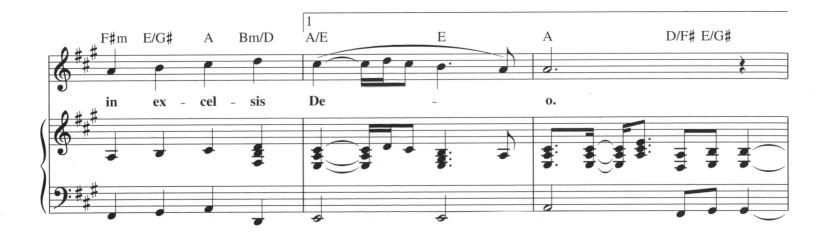

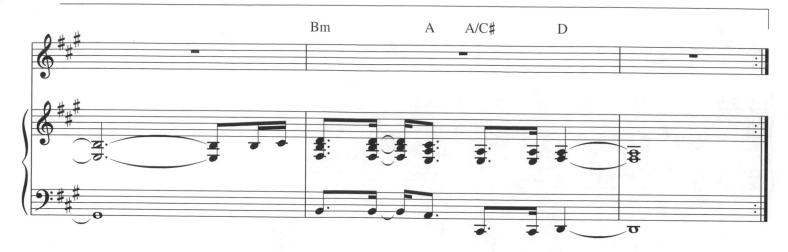

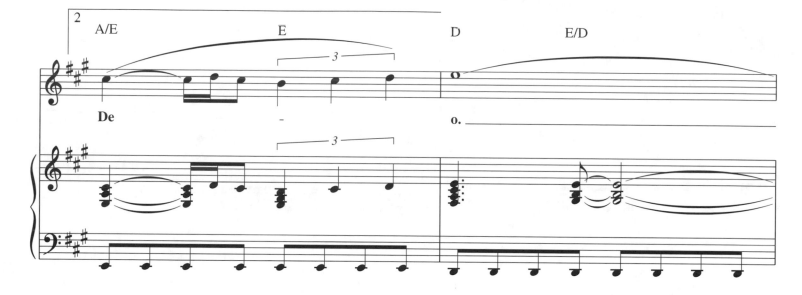

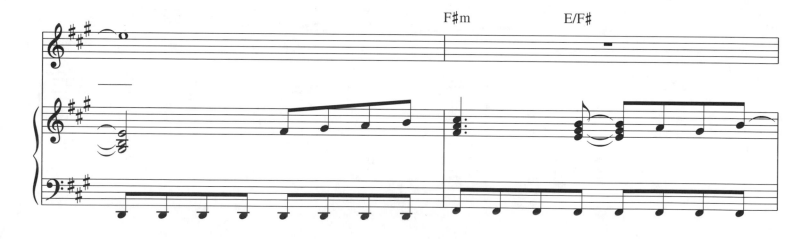

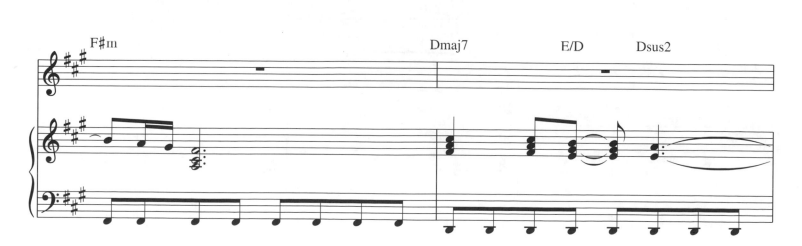

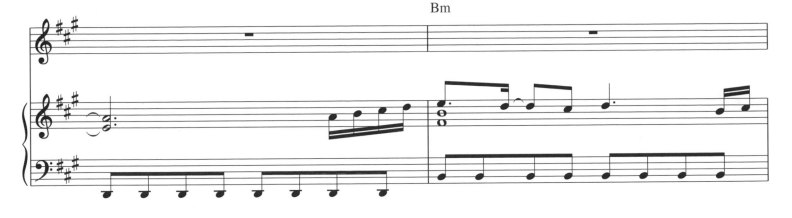

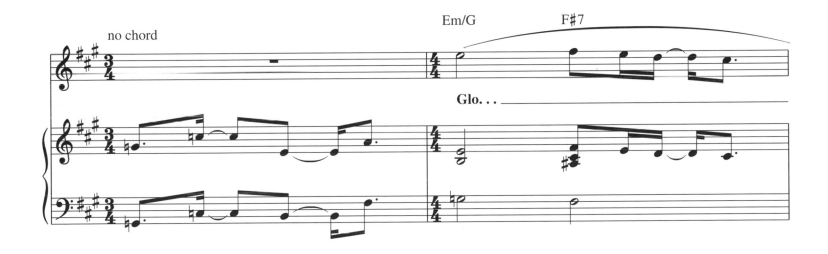

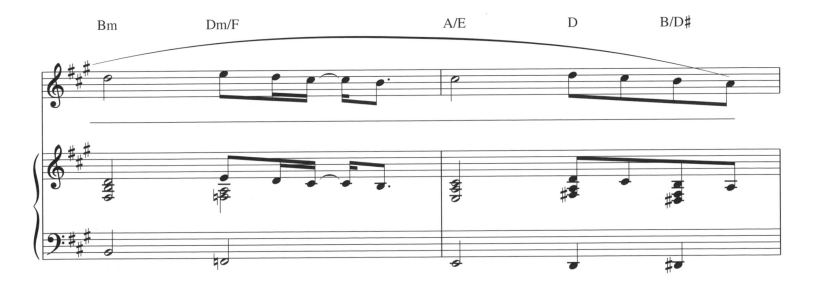

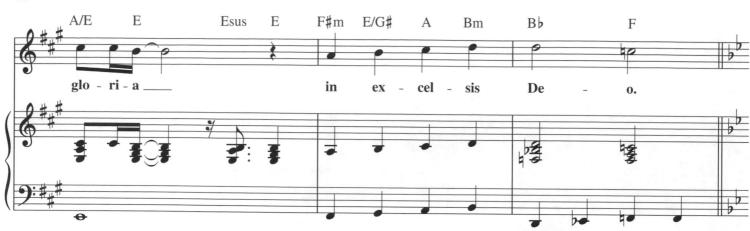

glo - ri - a _____ in ex - cel - sis De - o.

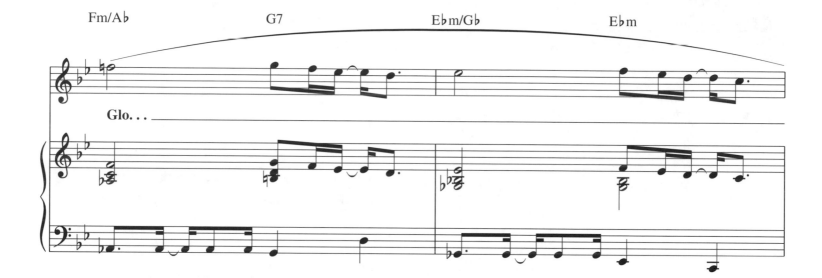

Glo. . . _____

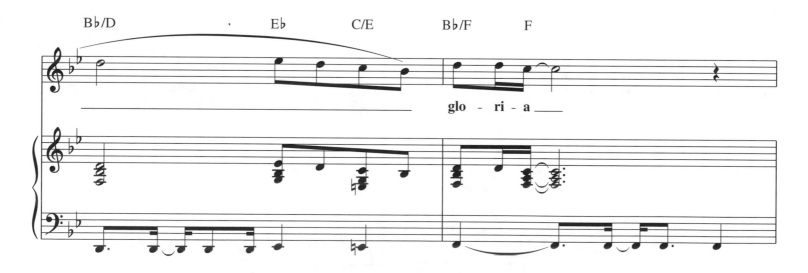

_____ glo - ri - a _____

in ex - cel - sis De - o, in ex - cel - sis

21

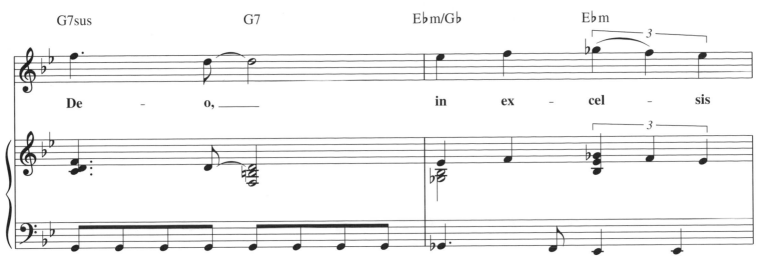

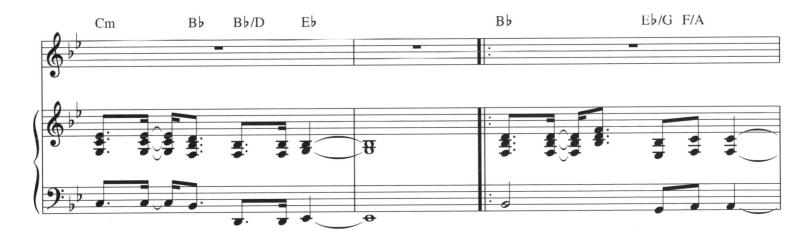

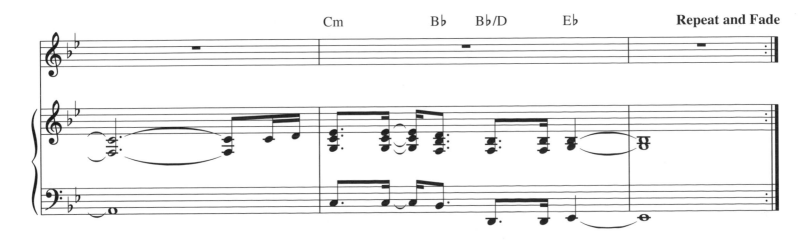

BE IT UNTO ME

Words and Music by RANDY PHILLIPS
and CINDY MORGAN

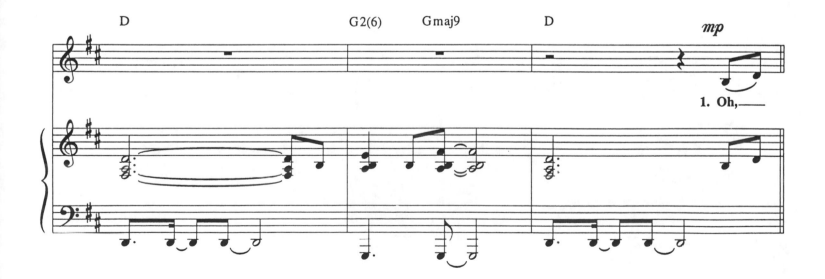

night you___ will car - ry___ the Sav - ior of___ the world.___
dy - ing,___ hear them cry - ing; bring a Sav - ior to___ their world.___

___ So will you go___ or___ will you stay?___ Then___ heav - en's an -
___ So will you go___ or___ will you stay?___ Don't___ you want heav -

- gel heard Ma - ry say:___ "Be it un - to me ac -
- en to hear you say:___

cord - ing to Your will, O Lord,___ O___ Lord. Be it un - to me ac -

D.S. al CODA %

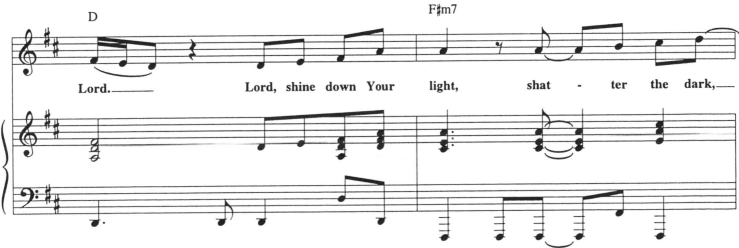

BETHLEHEM MORNING

Words and Music by
MORRIS CHAPMAN

prom - ise to ful - fill. _____

Je - ru - sa - lem, He cried _____

_____ for you, _____ He did not come to _ you

in vain. _____ His _____ lov - ing

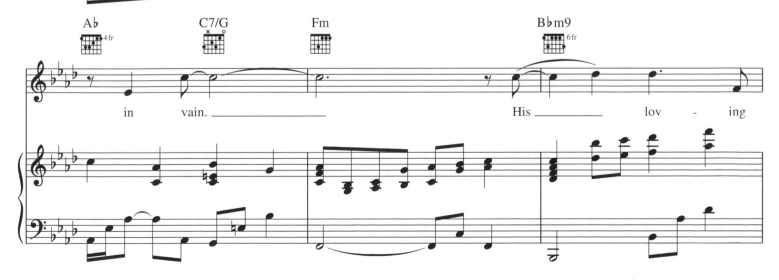

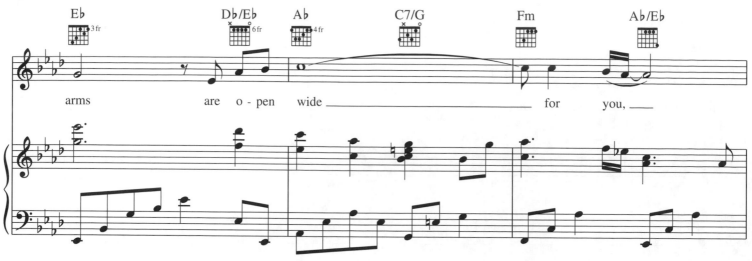

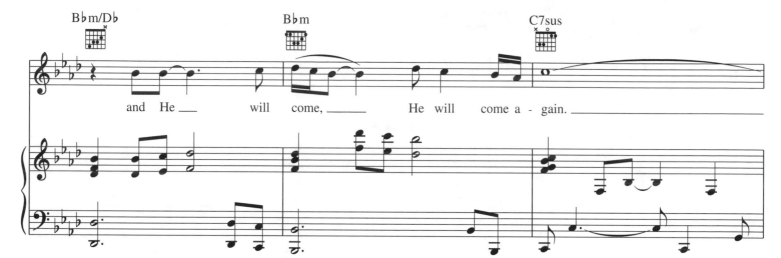

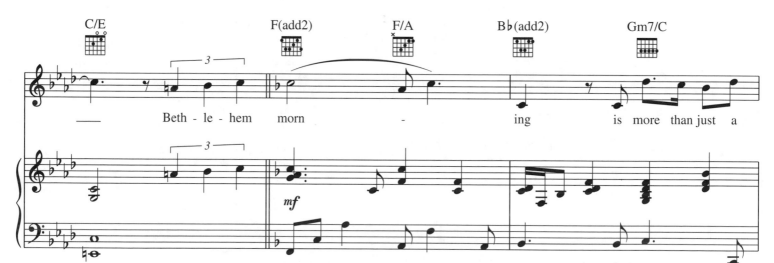

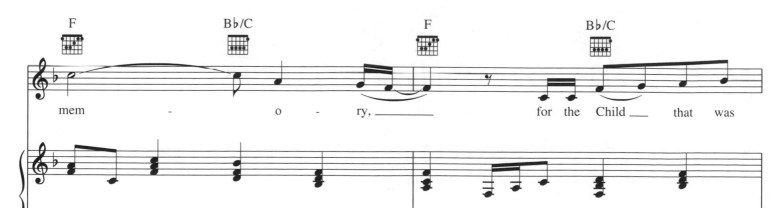

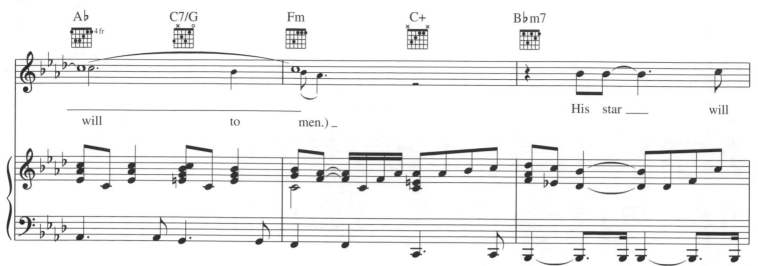

will _____ to men.) _

His star _____ will

nev-er, will nev-er grow dim, and it's ___ a ___

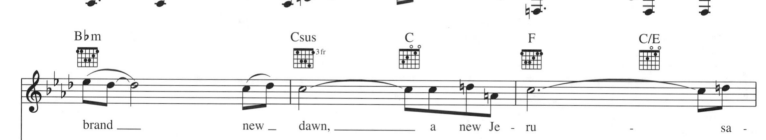

brand ___ new _ dawn, _____ a new Je - ru - sa -

lem, _____ and we, _____ and we will reign, we will reign

building

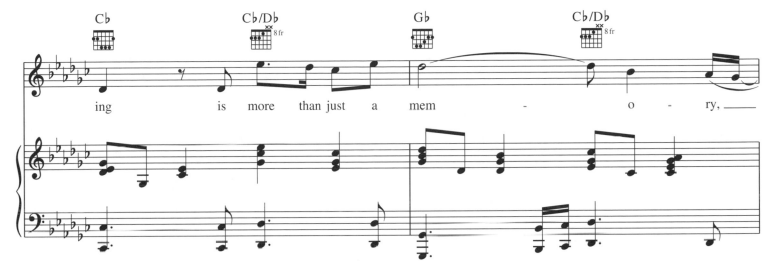

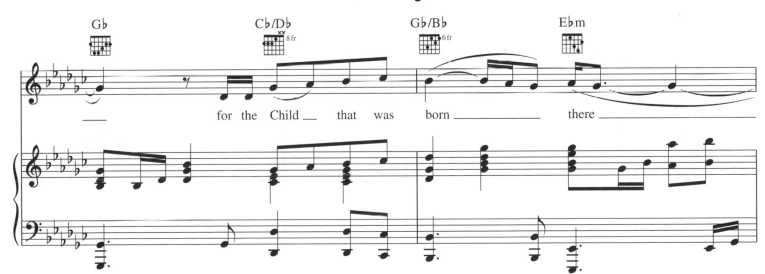

CALL HIS NAME JESUS

Words and Music by
SHAWN CRAIG

An an-gel came down to a vir-gin with a
no oth-er name that can save us, no

heav'n-ly word.
oth-er name.
The name of a beau-ti-ful prom-
No oth-er Lord can re-deem

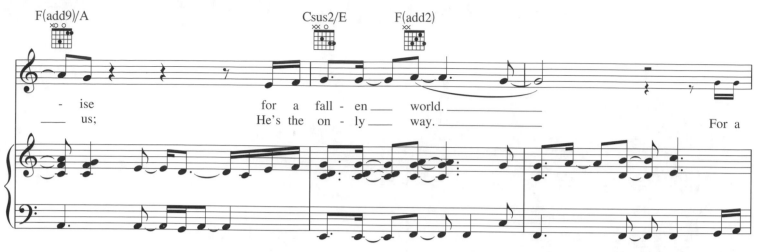

-ise
_____ us;

for a fall-en _____ world. _____
He's the on-ly _____ way. _____

For a

You will give birth _ to a Son, _____
Child has been giv-en for us, _____

the Child of the Most _ Ho-ly One.
a gift from the Fa-ther a-bove. __

_____ And they will call Him Won-der-ful,
_____ And we will call Him Won-der-ful,

Coun-sel-or,
Coun-sel-or,

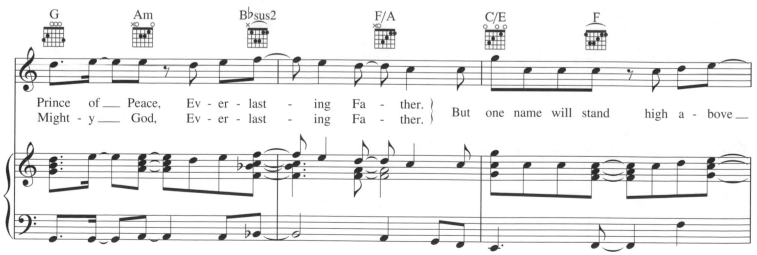

Prince of _ Peace, Ev-er-last-ing Fa-ther. }
Might-y _ God, Ev-er-last-ing Fa-ther. }

But one name will stand high a-bove __

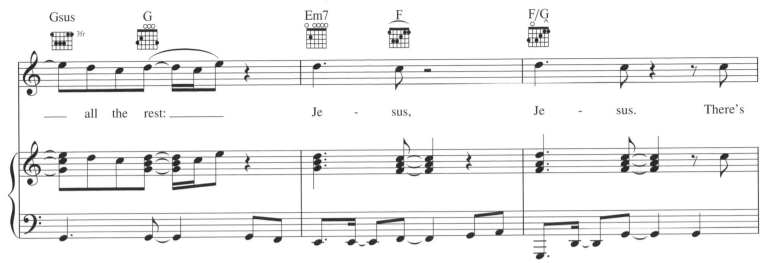

_____ all the rest: _____ Je - sus, Je - sus. There's

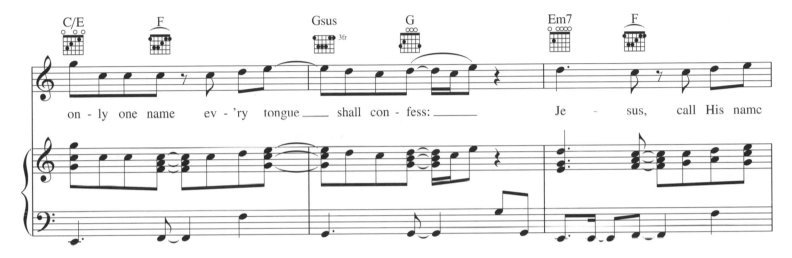

on - ly one name ev - 'ry tongue _____ shall con - fess: _____ Je - sus, call His name

Je - sus.

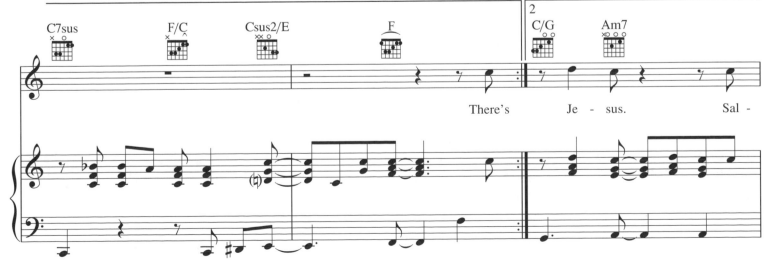

There's Je - sus. Sal -

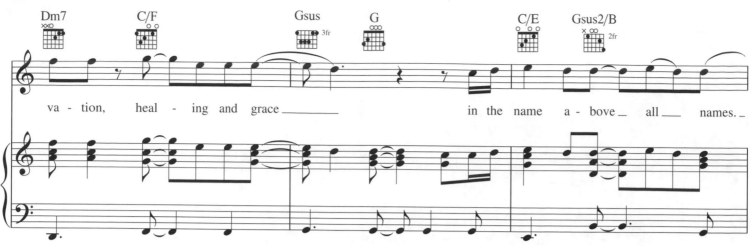

va - tion, heal - ing and grace _____ in the name a - bove _ all __ names. _

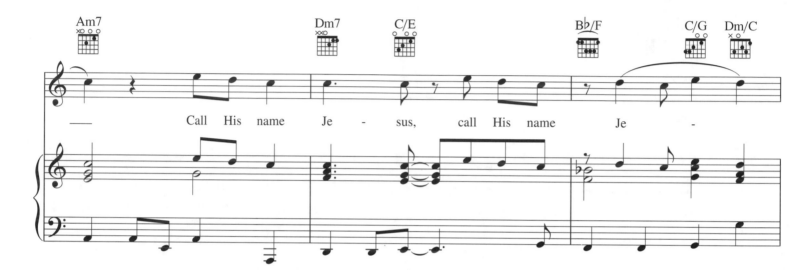

__ Call His name Je - sus, call His name Je -

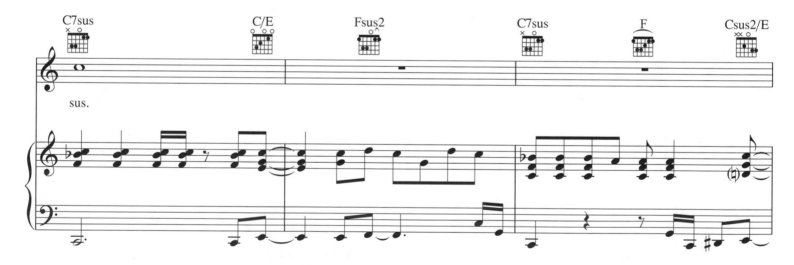

sus.

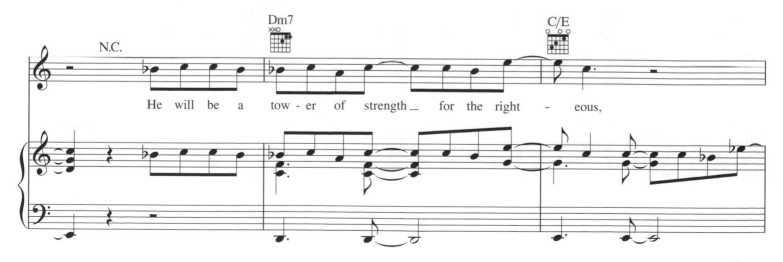

He will be a tow - er of strength _ for the right - eous,

might-y ref-uge from the storm ____ that rag - es. Ev - 'ry knee __ shall

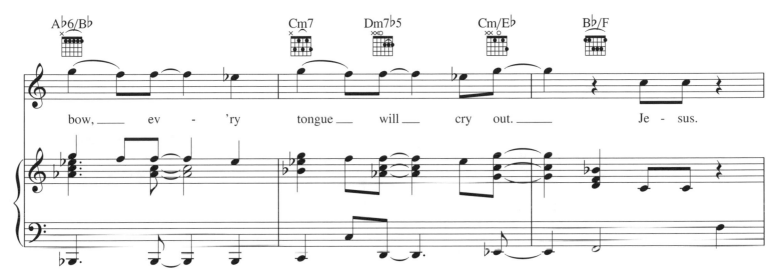

bow, ___ ev - 'ry tongue __ will __ cry out. ___ Je - sus.

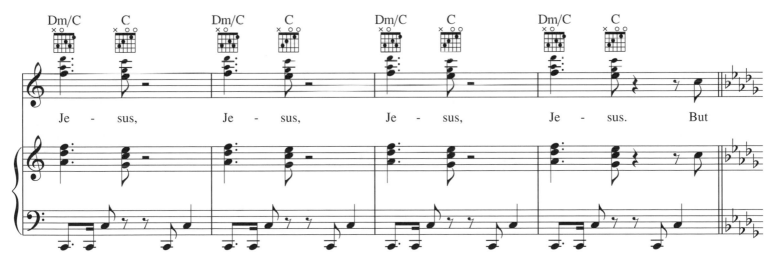

Je - sus, Je - sus, Je - sus, Je - sus. But

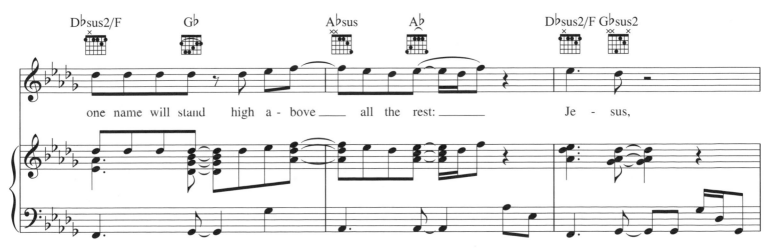

one name will stand high a - bove ___ all the rest: ___ Je - sus,

Je - sus. There's on - ly one name ev - 'ry tongue ___ shall con - fess: ___

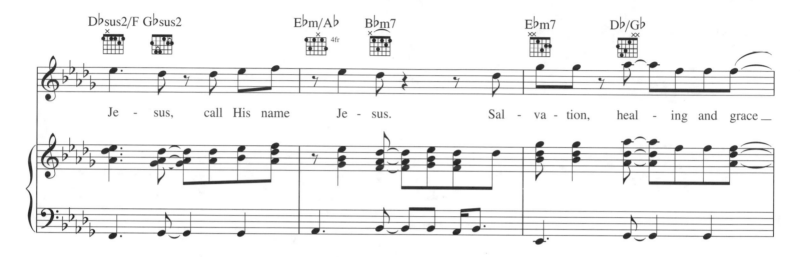

Je - sus, call His name Je - sus. Sal - va - tion, heal - ing and grace ___

___ in the name a - bove ___ all ___ names. ___ Call His name

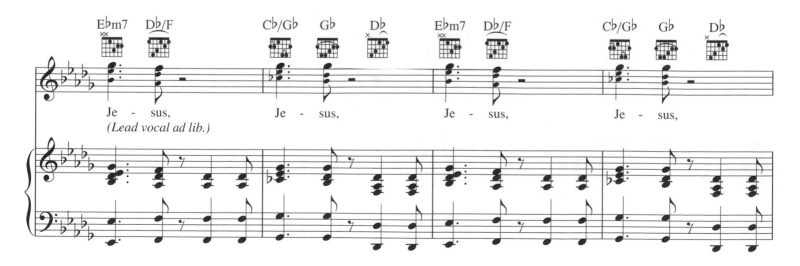

Je - sus, Je - sus, Je - sus, Je - sus,

(Lead vocal ad lib.)

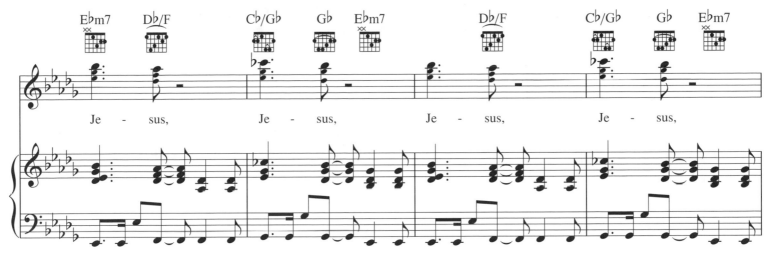

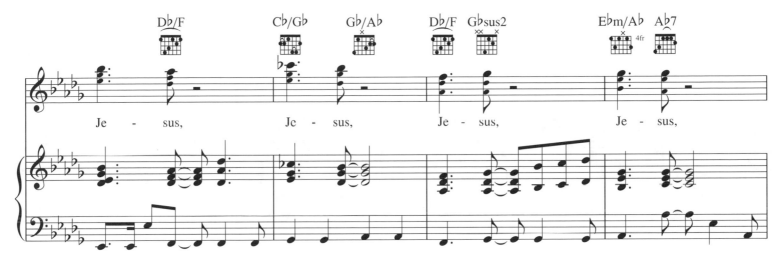

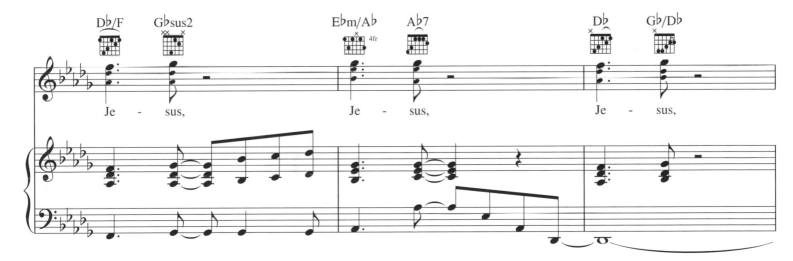

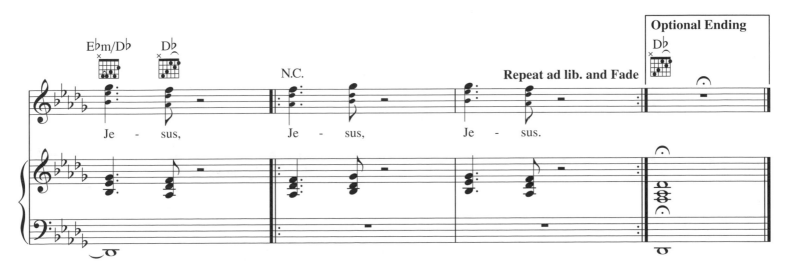

BREATH OF HEAVEN
(Mary's Song)

Words and Music by AMY GRANT
and CHRIS EATON

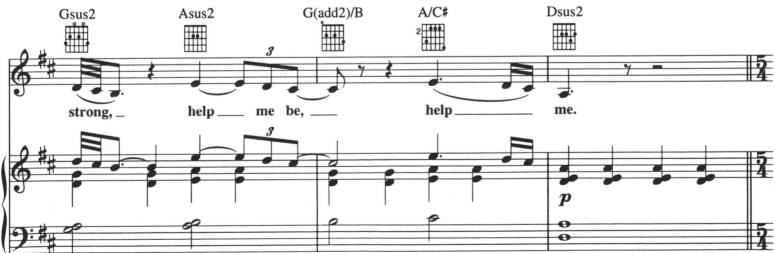

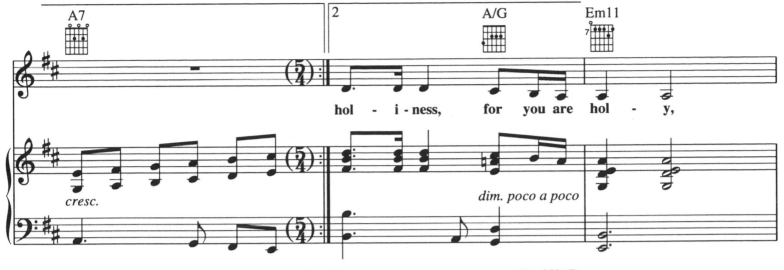

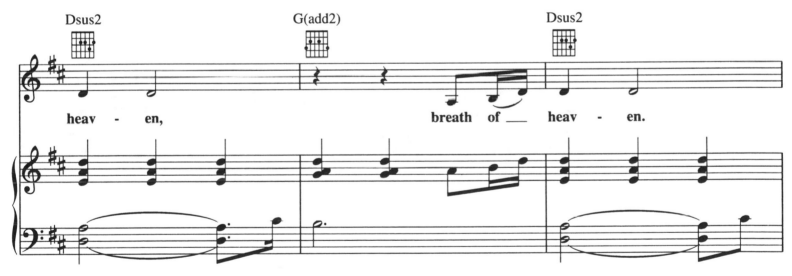

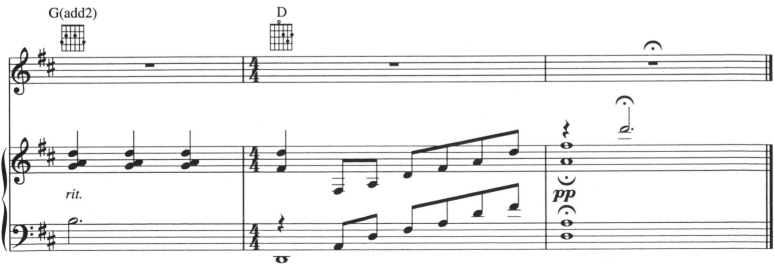

CAROL OF THE BELLS

Ukrainian Christmas Carol
Arranged by STEVEN CURTIS CHAPMAN

Moderately fast

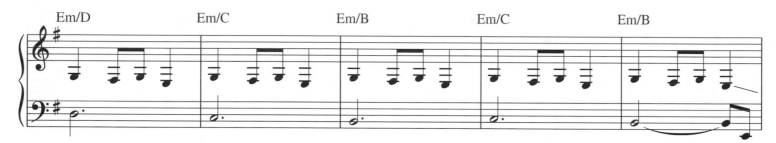

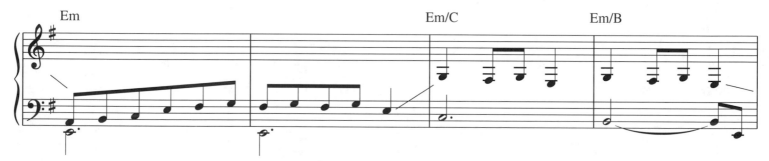

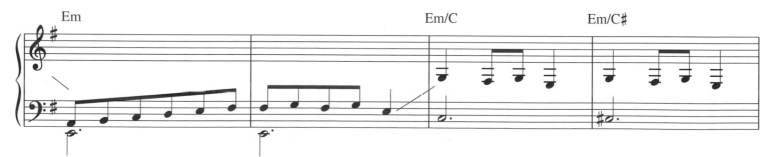

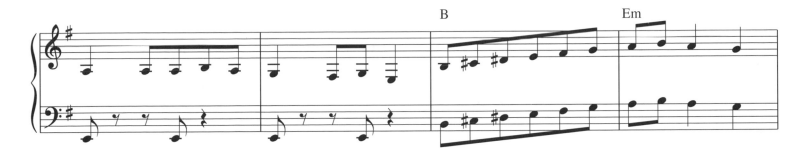

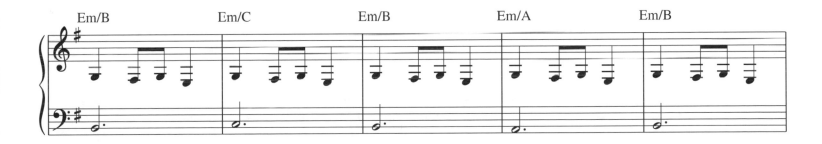

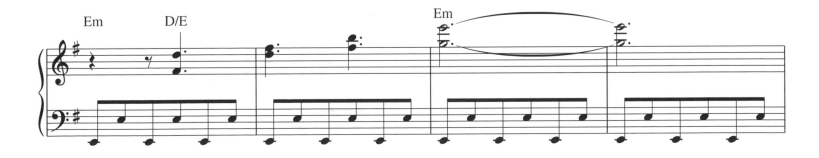

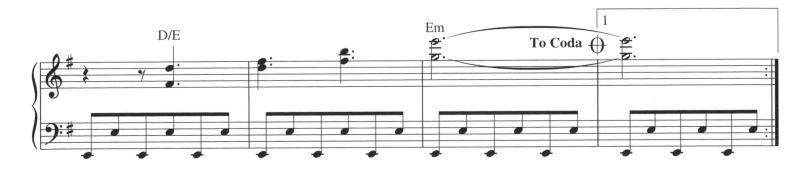

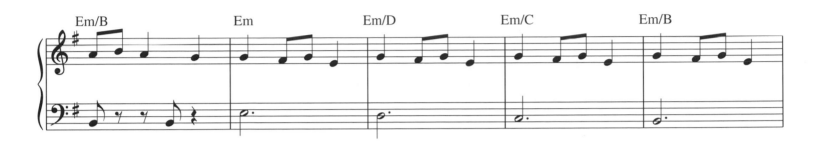

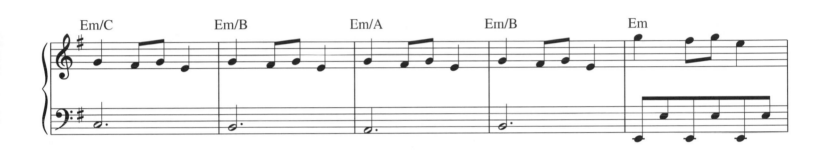

CELEBRATE THE CHILD

Words and Music by
MICHAEL CARD

In four with a beat

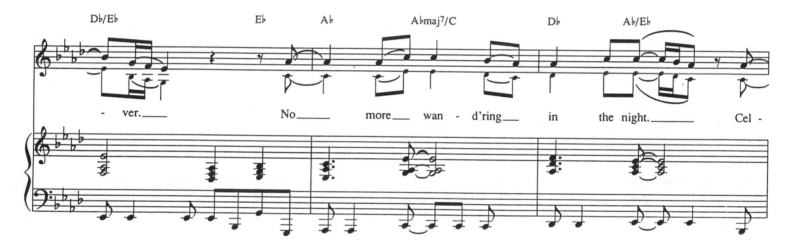

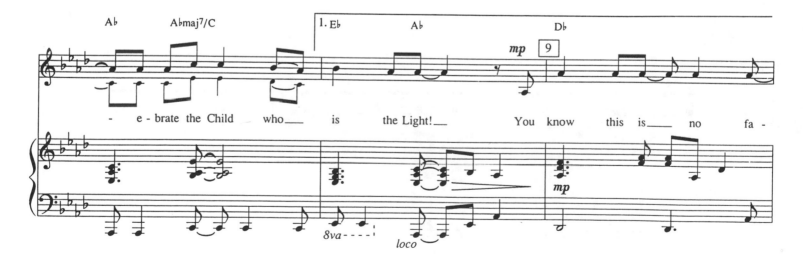

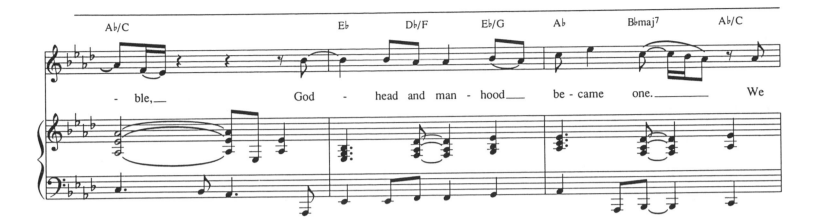

-ble,___ God - head and man - hood___ be - came one.___ We

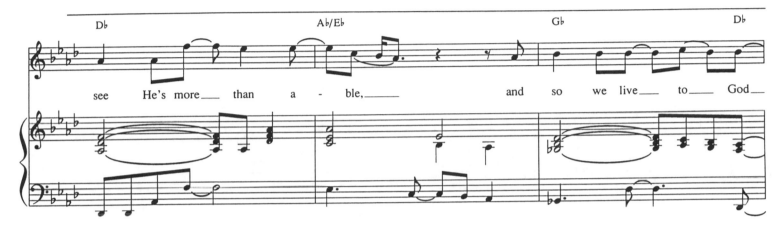

see He's more___ than a - ble,___ and so we live___ to___ God___

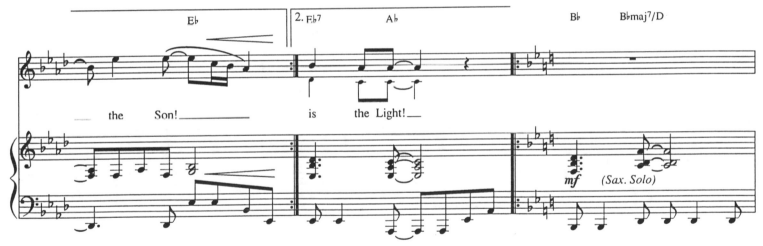

___ the Son!___ is the Light!___

(Sax. Solo)

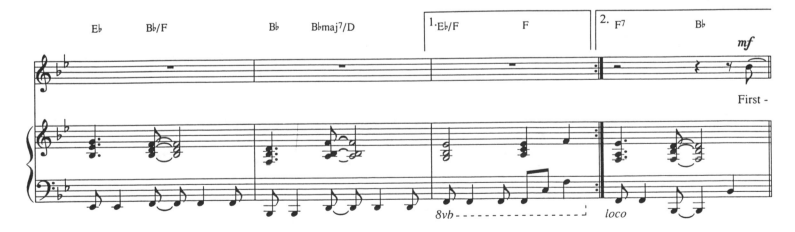

First -

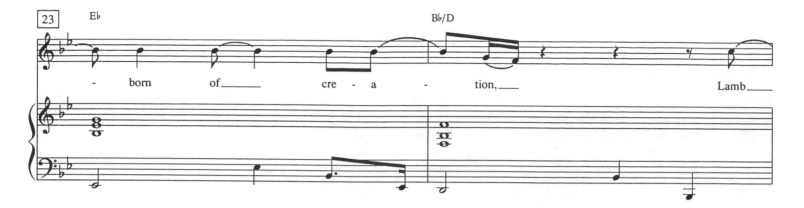

born of_____ cre - a - tion,_____ Lamb_____

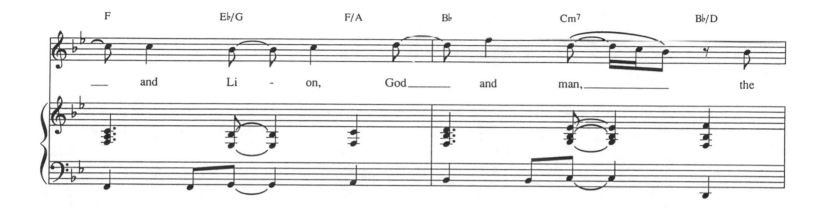

_____ and Li - on, God_____ and man,_____ the

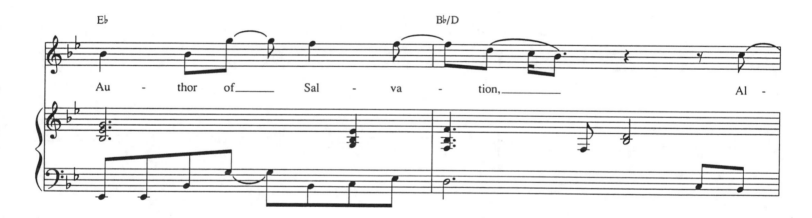

Au - thor of_____ Sal - va - tion,_____ Al -

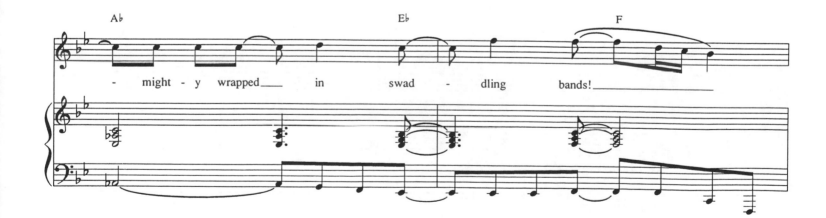

- might - y wrapped_____ in swad - dling bands!_____

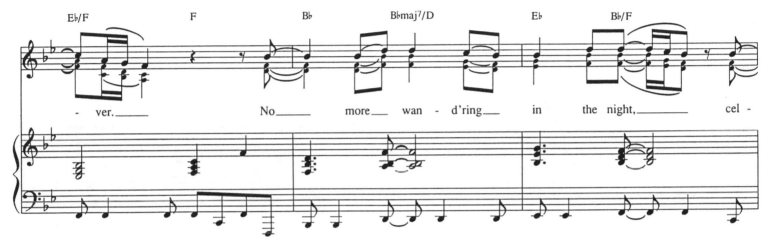

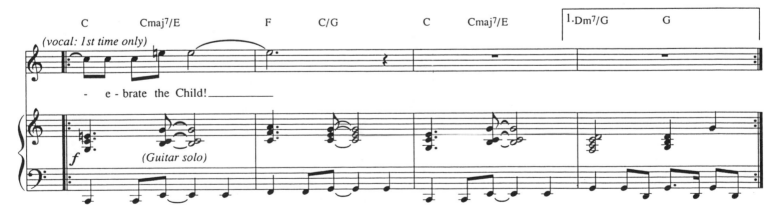

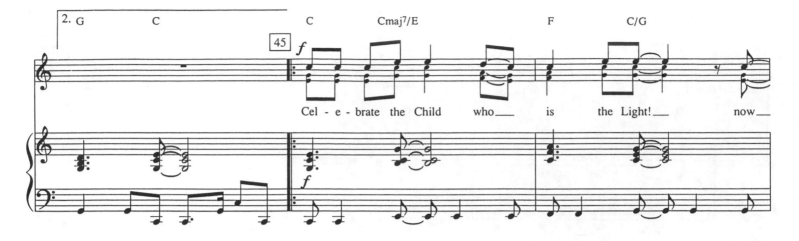

Cel - e - brate the Child who____ is the Light!____ now____

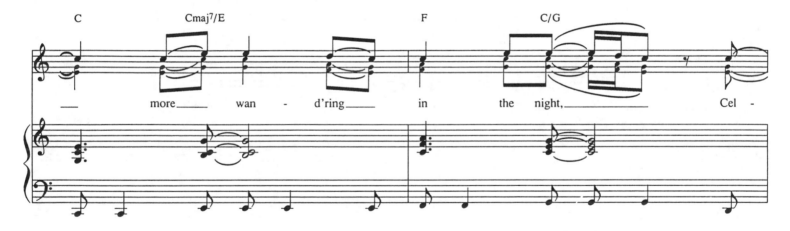

____ the dark - ness is____ o - ver.____ No____

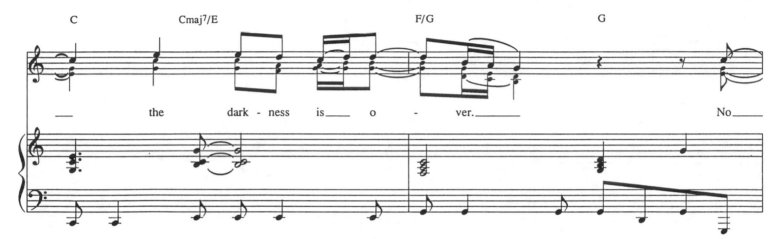

____ more____ wan - d'ring____ in the night,_____ Cel -

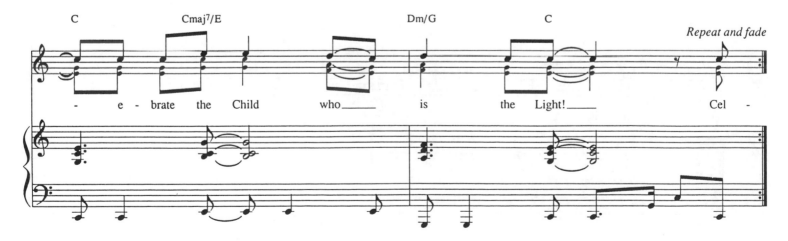

Repeat and fade

- e - brate the Child who____ is the Light!____ Cel -

A CRADLE PRAYER

Words and Music by REBECCA ST. JAMES
and CHARLES GARRETT

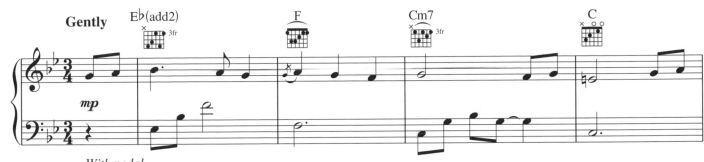

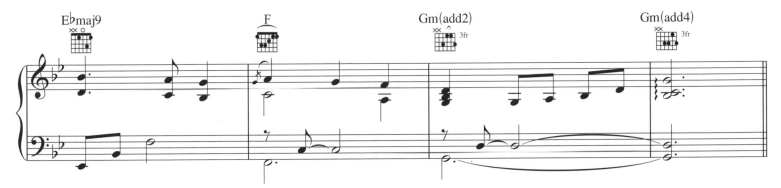

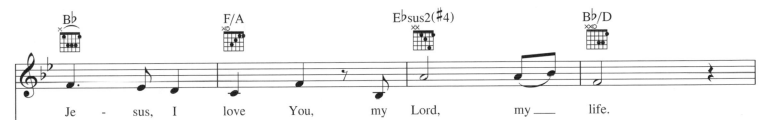

Je - sus, I love You, my Lord, my ___ life.

Where would I be with - out You?

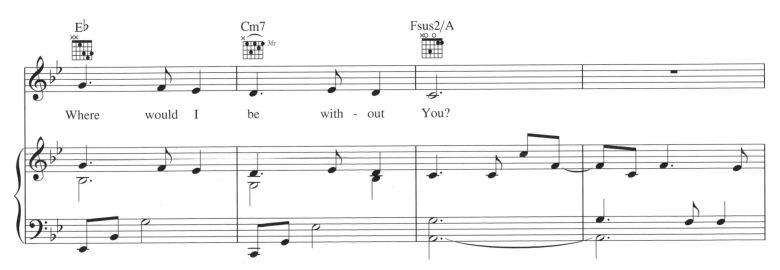

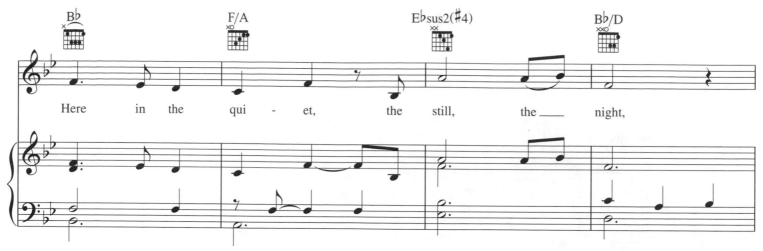

Here in the qui - et, the still, the ___ night,

I am in awe of You. ___

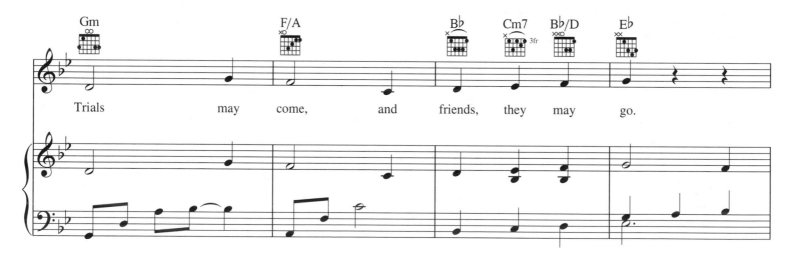

Trials may come, and friends, they may go.

What real - ly mat - ters is You, my ___ Lord.

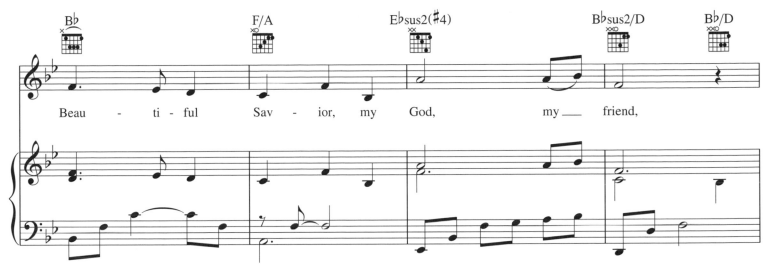

Beau - ti - ful Sav - ior, my God, my __ friend,

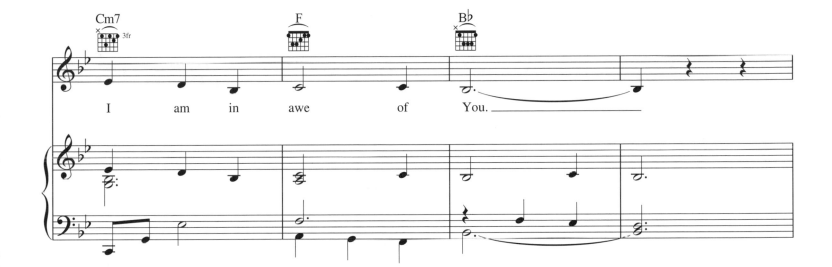

I am in awe of You. _____

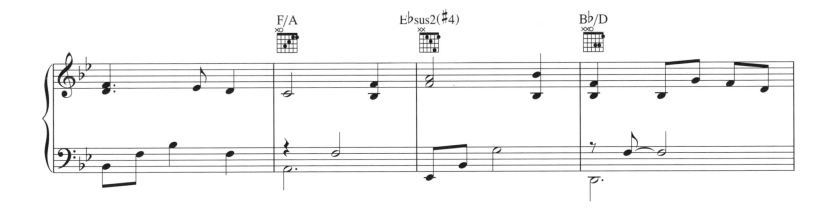

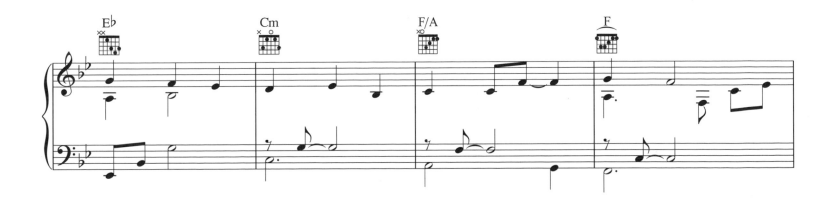

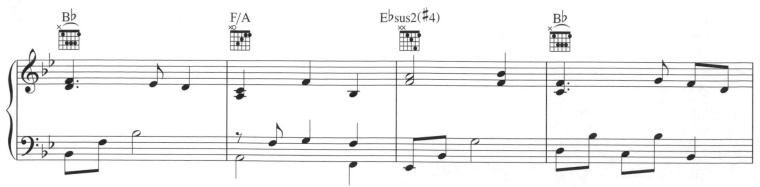

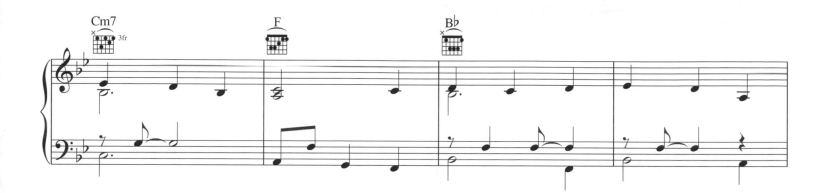

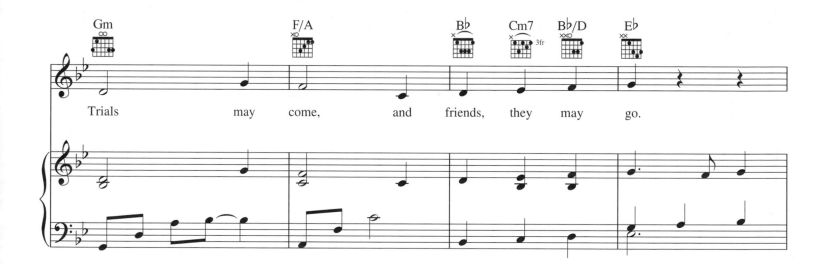

Trials may come, and friends, they may go.

What real-ly mat-ters is You, my __ Lord. _____

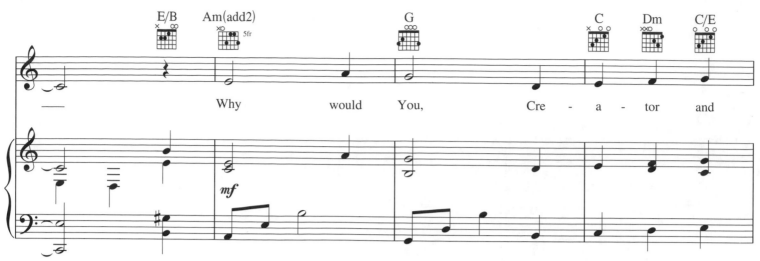

Why would You, Cre - a - tor and

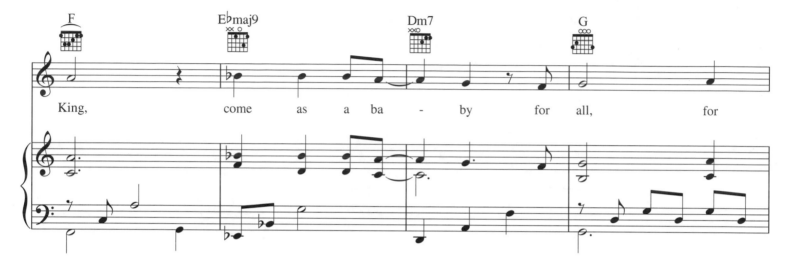

King, come as a ba - by for all, for

me? Beau - ti - ful

Sav - ior, my God, my friend, I am in

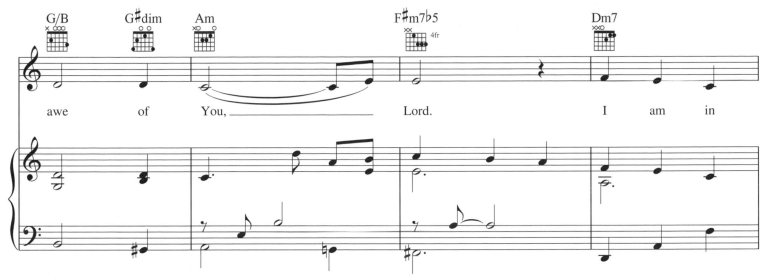

awe   of   You, _____ Lord.   I   am   in

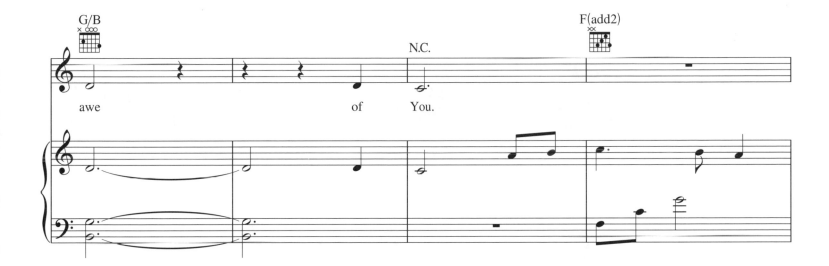

awe   of   You.

CHILD OF BETHLEHEM

Words by WAYNE WATSON and CLAIRE CLONINGER
Music by WAYNE WATSON

from their____ sleep. And the heavn's re -

joice! And the an - gels sing! The____

Child of Beth - le - hem is the King of____

kings!

Down from heav - en's glo - ry, to a__ man - ger

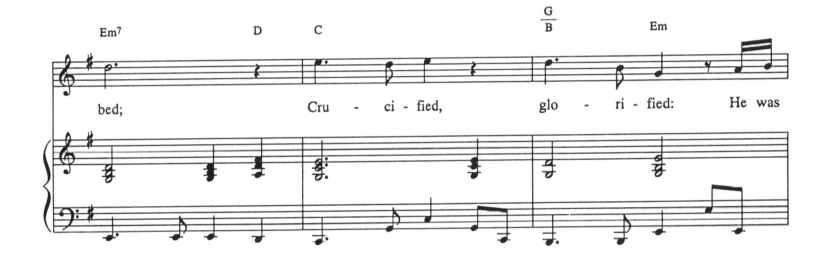

bed; Cru - ci - fied, glo - ri - fied: He was

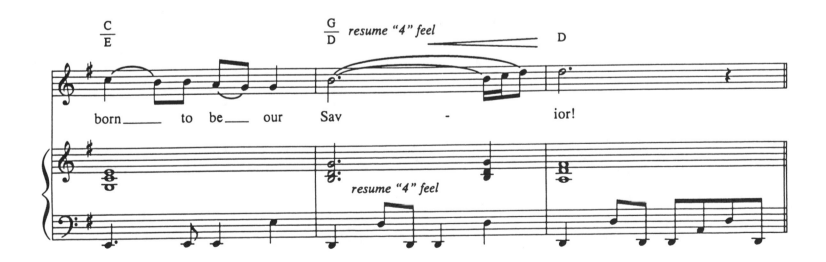

born__ to be__ our Sav - ior!

CHRISTMAS IS ALL IN THE HEART

Words and Music by
STEVEN CURTIS CHAPMAN

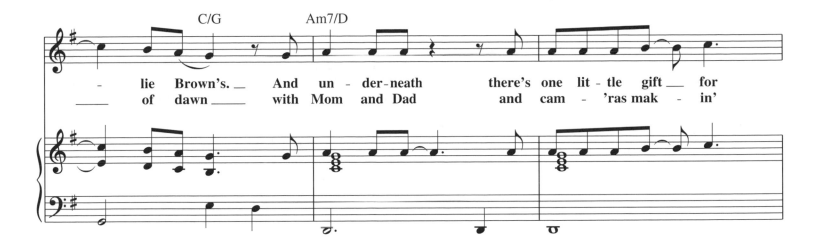

-lie Brown's. ___ And un-der-neath there's one lit-tle gift ___ for
___ of dawn ___ with Mom and Dad and cam-'ras mak-in'

him, and one lit-tle gift ___ for her. ___
sure we'd nev-er for-get ___ that day. ___

Af-ter six months on ___ the new ___
Now I'm the one who's tak ___ in' pic -

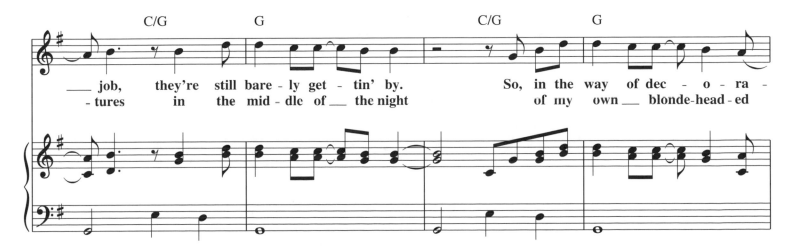

___ job, they're still bare-ly get-tin' by. So, in the way of dec-o-ra-
-tures in the mid-dle of ___ the night of my own ___ blonde-head-ed

in _____ the heart, _____ that's where _____ the feel - ing starts _____

_____ and like _____ a fire _____ in - side, _____ it

touch - es ev - 'ry part, _____ 'cause Christ - mas _____ is all _____

_____ in _____ the _____ heart. And e ven _____ if _____

Two lit-tle ___ No, it's

not ___ in ___ the snow ___ that may or may ___ not fall. ___

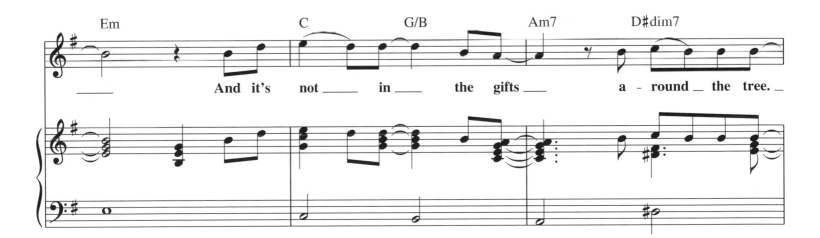

And it's not ___ in ___ the gifts ___ a - round ___ the tree.

It's in the love heav - en gave ___ the

night our Sav - ior came. And that _ same Love _ can still be found _

_ wher - ev - er you are _____ 'cause

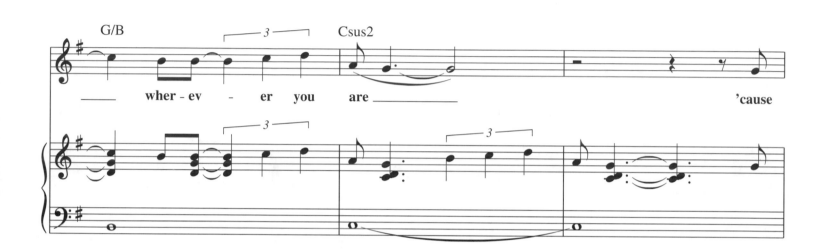

Christ - mas _ is all ____ in ___ the heart. _ And the joy _

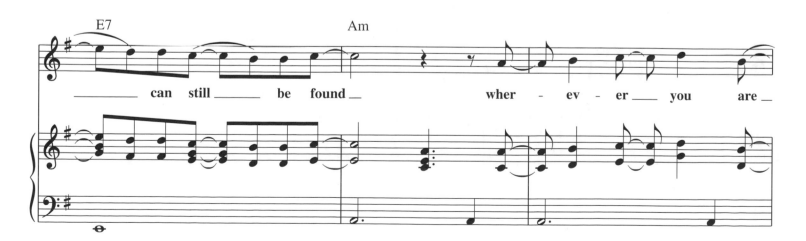

___ can still ____ be found _ wher - ev - er __ you are _

'cause Christ - mas __ is all, _____

all in ___ the ___ heart. __

It's all in ___ the ___ heart. __

rit.

THE CHRISTMAS SHOES

Words and Music by LEONARD AHLSTROM
and EDDIE CARSWELL

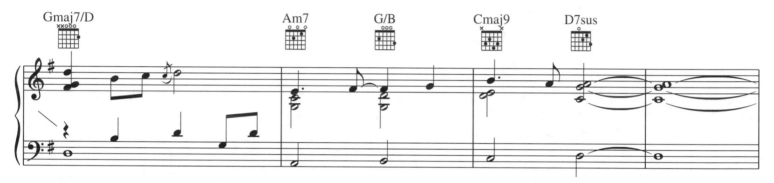

It was al - most Christ - mas time; ___ there I stood in an -

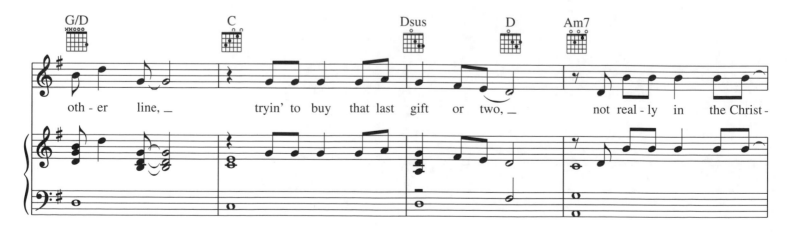

oth - er line, ___ tryin' to buy that last gift or two, ___ not real - ly in the Christ -

- mas mood. __ Stand-in' right in front __ of me was a lit - tle boy wait-ing

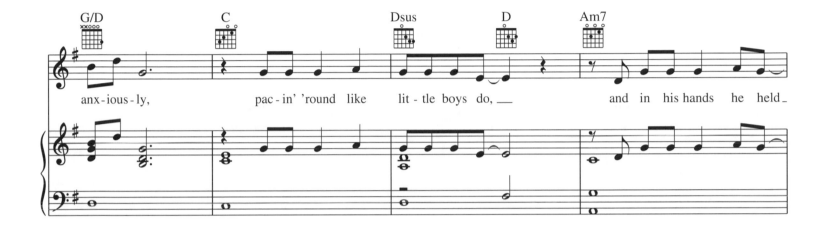

anx-ious-ly, pac-in' 'round like lit - tle boys do, __ and in his hands he held __

__ a pair of shoes. And his clothes were worn and old, __

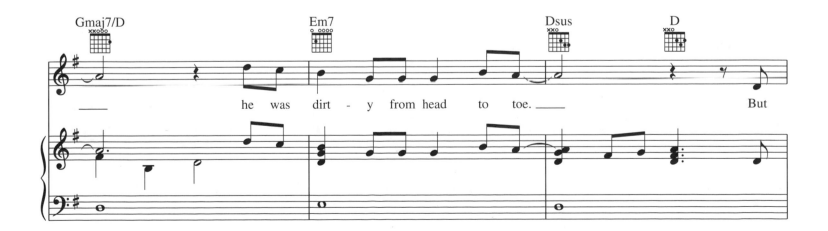

__ he was dirt - y from head to toe. __ But

when it came __ his time __ to pay, __ I could-n't be - lieve __ what I heard him say.

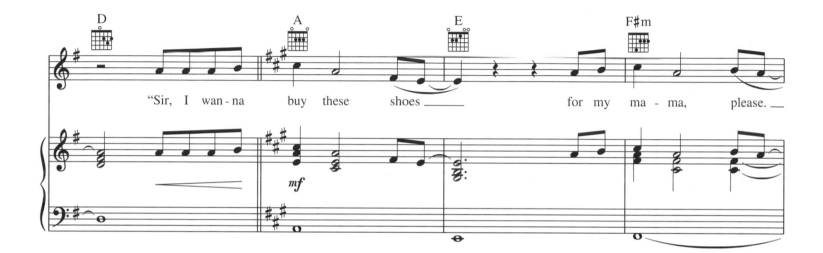

"Sir, I wan - na buy these shoes _____ for my ma - ma, please. __

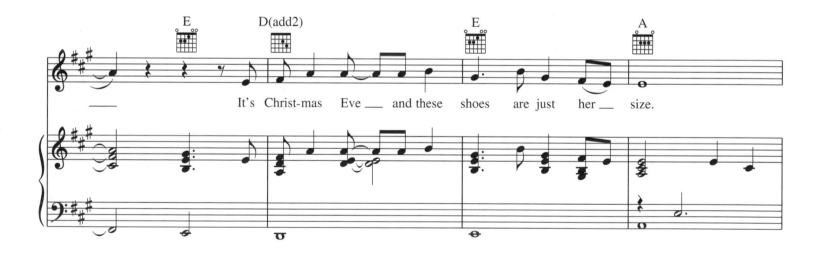

__ It's Christ-mas Eve __ and these shoes are just her __ size.

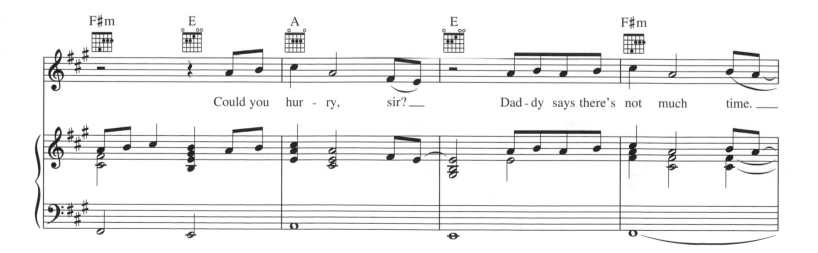

Could you hur - ry, sir? __ Dad - dy says there's not much time. __

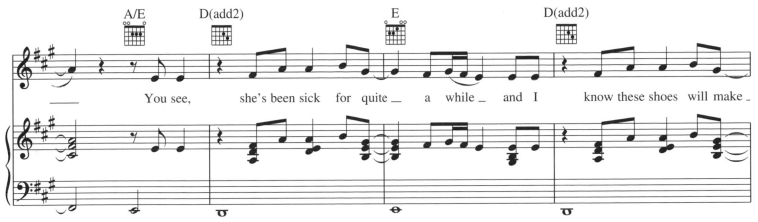

You see, she's been sick for quite __ a while __ and I know these shoes will make __

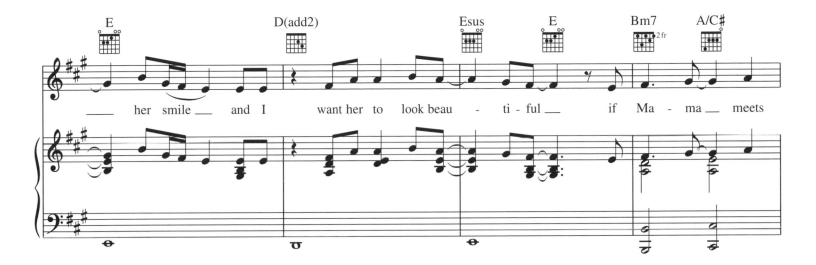

__ her smile __ and I want her to look beau - ti - ful __ if Ma - ma __ meets

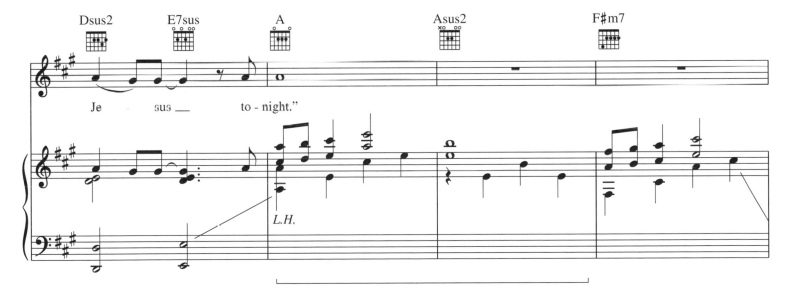

Je - sus __ to - night."

L.H.

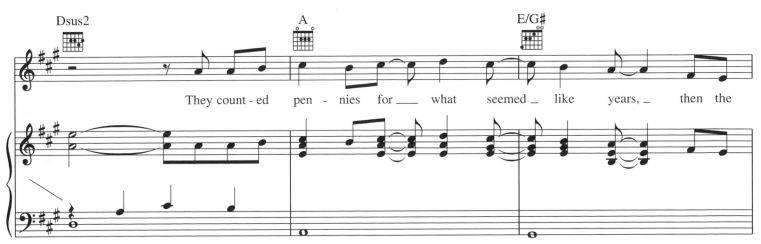

They count - ed pen - nies for __ what seemed __ like years, __ then the

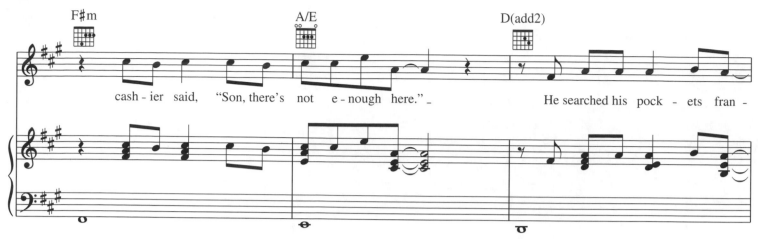

cash - ier said, "Son, there's not e - nough here." _ He searched his pock - ets fran -

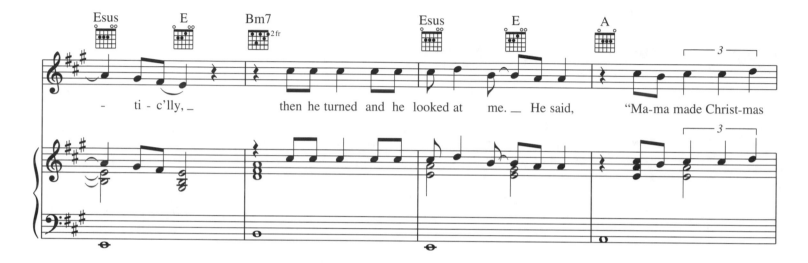

- ti - c'lly, _ then he turned and he looked at me. _ He said, "Ma-ma made Christ-mas

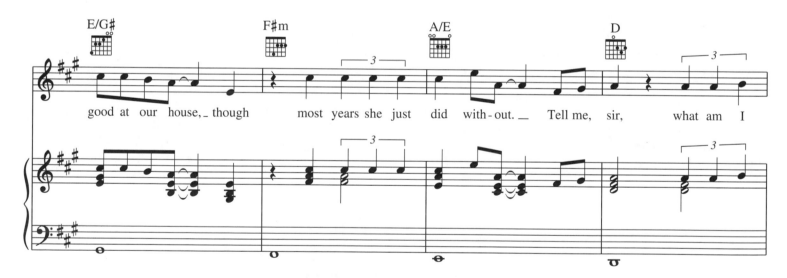

good at our house, _ though most years she just did with - out. _ Tell me, sir, what am I

gon - na do? ___ Some - how I've got - ta buy ___ her these Christ - mas

shoes." So, I laid the mon - ey down. ___ I just

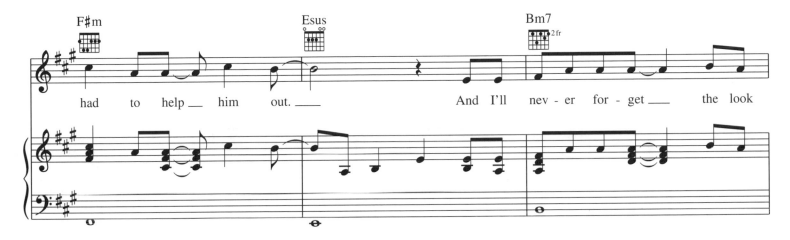

had to help ___ him out. ___ And I'll nev - er for - get ___ the look

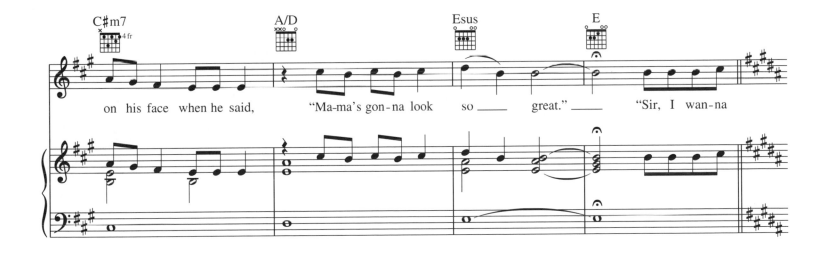

on his face when he said, "Ma-ma's gon-na look so ___ great." ___ "Sir, I wan-na

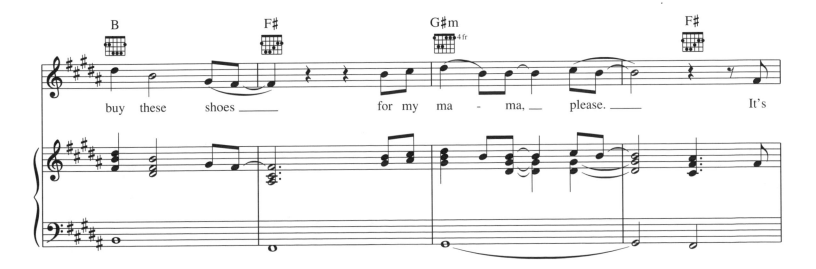

buy these shoes ___ for my ma - ma, ___ please. ___ It's

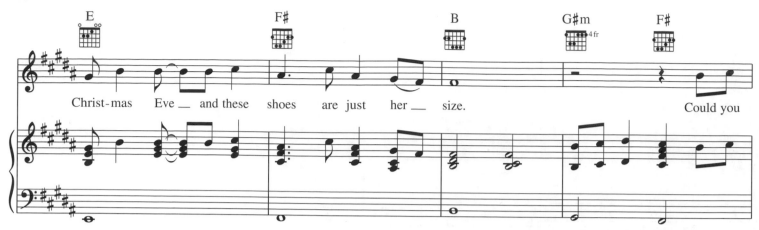

Christ-mas Eve __ and these shoes are just her __ size. Could you

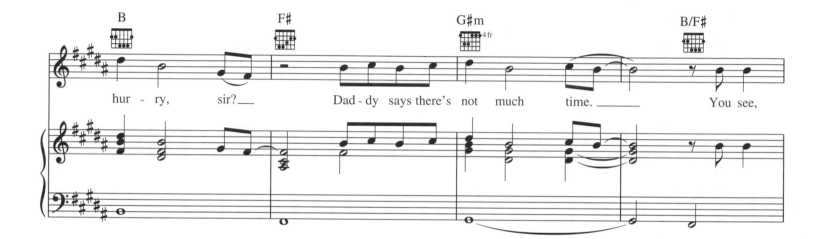

hur - ry, sir?__ Dad-dy says there's not much time. _____ You see,

she's been sick for quite __ a while __ and I know these shoes will make __

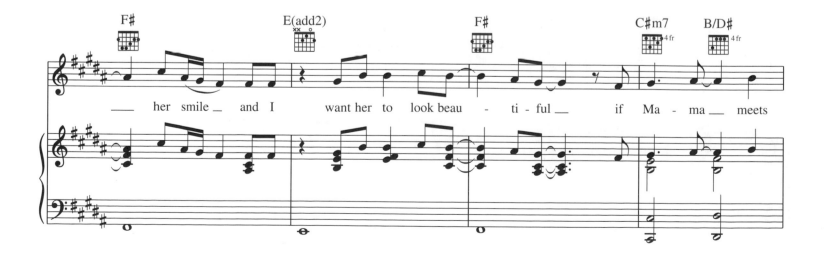

__ her smile __ and I want her to look beau - ti - ful __ if Ma - ma __ meets

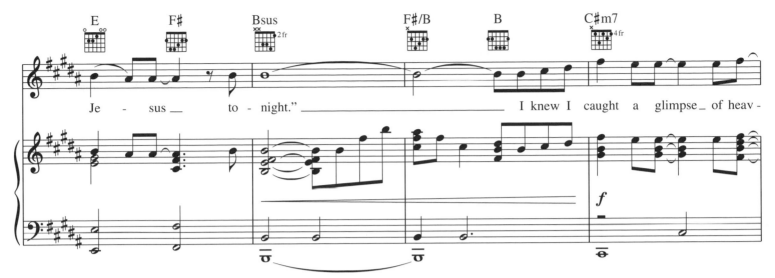

Je - sus ___ to - night." _____ I knew I caught a glimpse ___ of heav -

- en's love ___ as he thanked me and ___ ran out. ___ I knew that

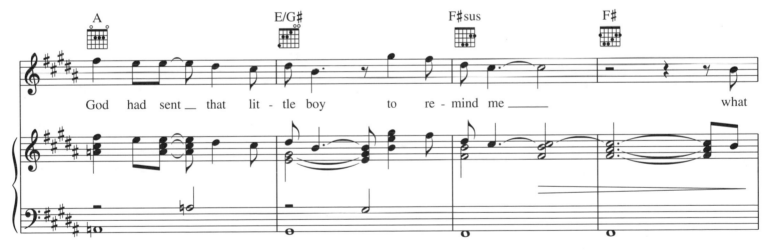

God had sent ___ that lit - tle boy to re - mind me _____ what

Christ - mas is all a - bout. *Children:* "Sir, I wan - na buy these shoes ___

for my ma - ma, please. ___ It's Christ-mas Eve ___ and these

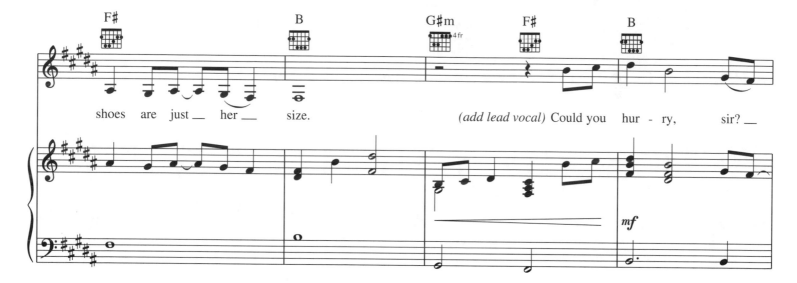

shoes are just ___ her ___ size. *(add lead vocal)* Could you hur - ry, sir? ___

Dad-dy says there's not much time. ___ You see, she's been sick for quite ___

___ a while ___ and I know these shoes will make ___ her smile ___ and I

want her to look beau - ti - ful ___ if Ma - ma ___ meets Je - sus ___ to -

night. *Boy:* I want her to ___ look beau - ti - ful if

Ma - ma ___ meets Je - sus ___ to - night." ___

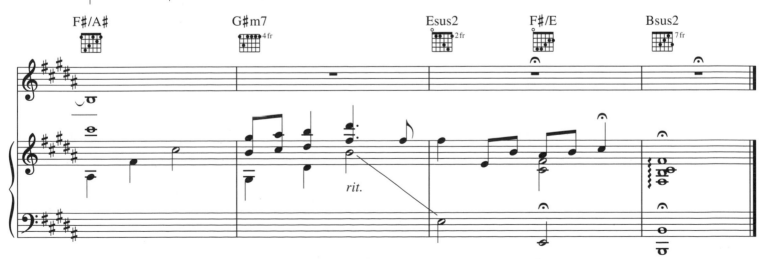

COME, THOU LONG EXPECTED JESUS

Arranged by
J.A.C. REDFORD

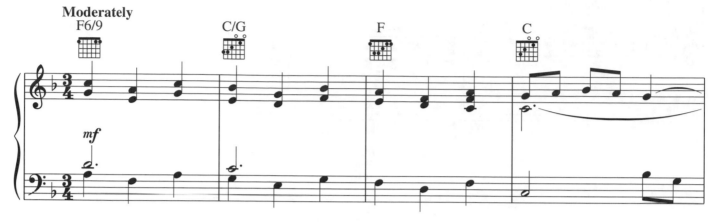

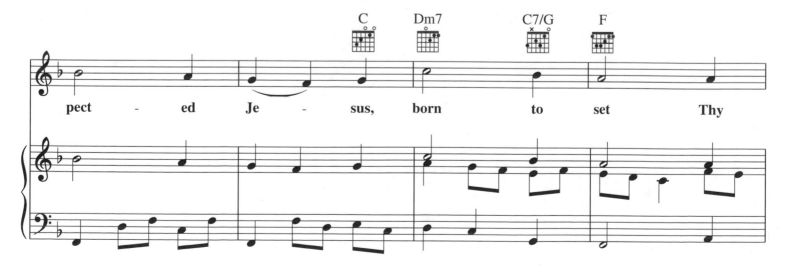

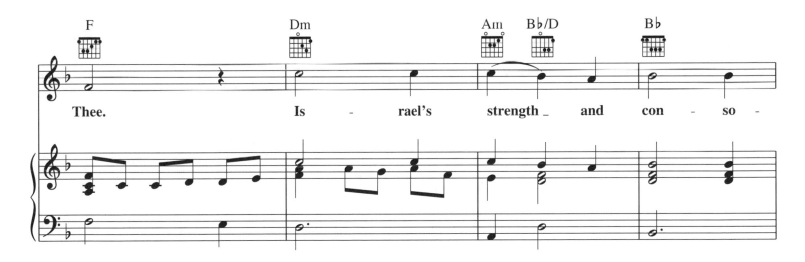

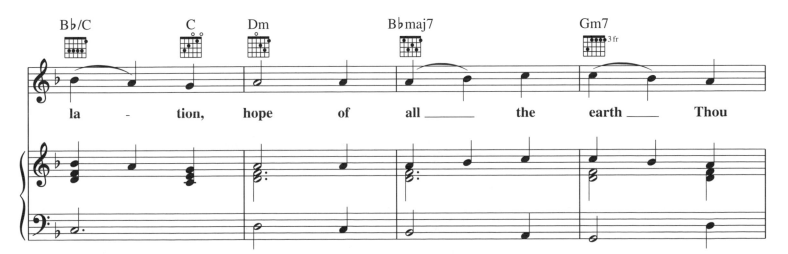

art. Dear _____ de - sire _____ of ev - 'ry

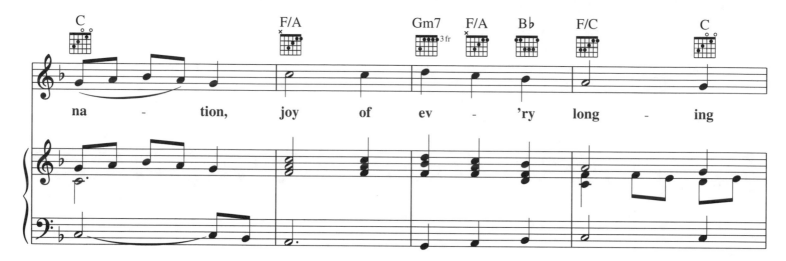

na - tion, joy of ev - 'ry long - ing

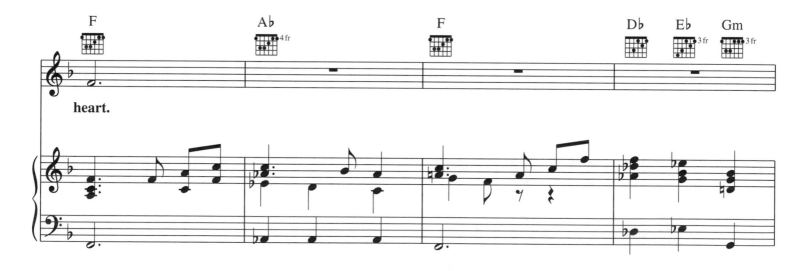

heart.

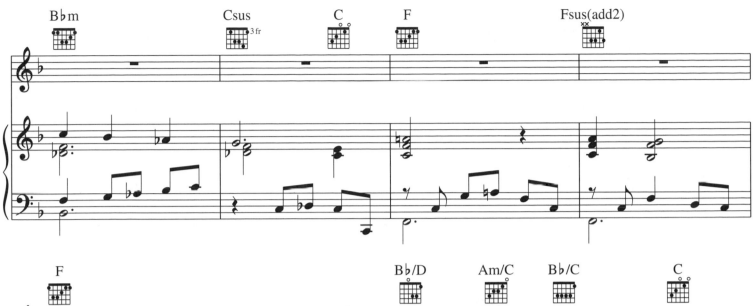

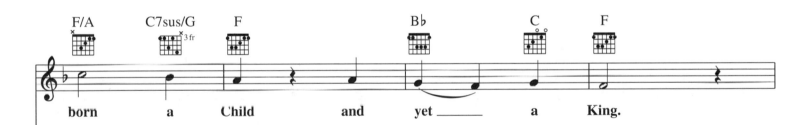

Born Thy peo - ple to de - liv - er,

born a Child and yet _____ a King.

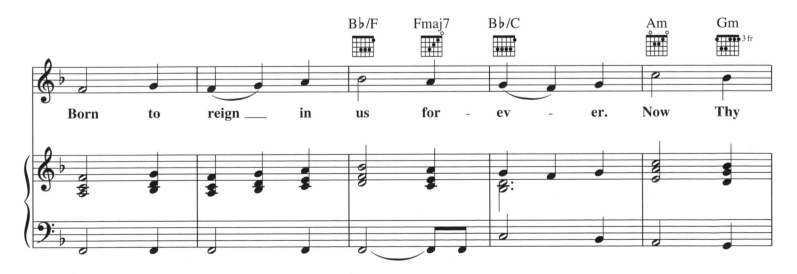

Born to reign ___ in us for - ev - er. Now Thy

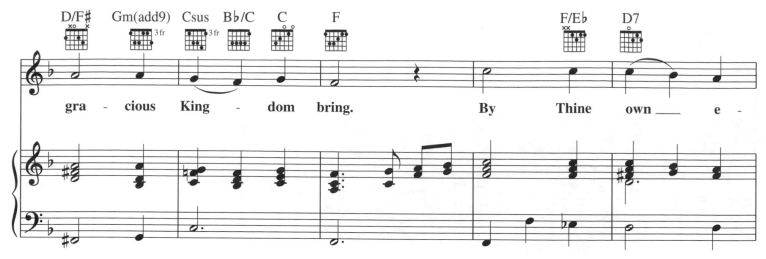

gra - cious King - dom bring. By Thine own ___ e -

ter - nal spir - it, rule in all ___ our

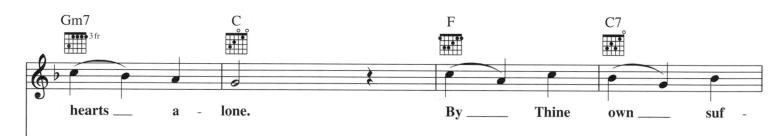

hearts ___ a - lone. By ___ Thine own ___ suf -

fi - cient mer - it, raise us to ___ Thy

glo - rious throne.

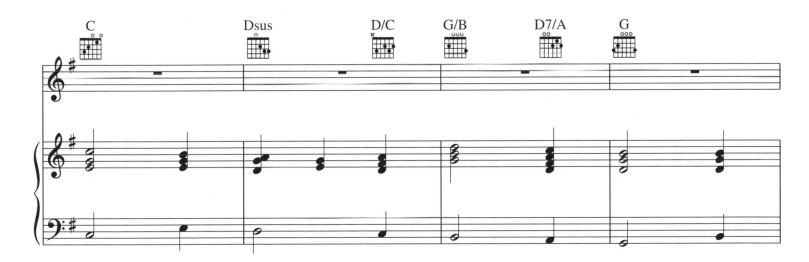

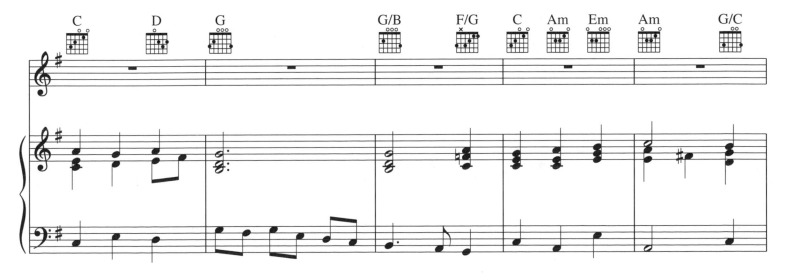

By Thine own _____ e - ter - nal

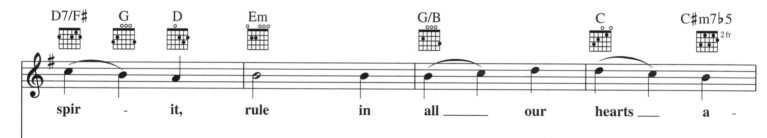

spir - it, rule in all _____ our hearts ___ a -

lone. By _____ Thine own _____ suf - fi - cient

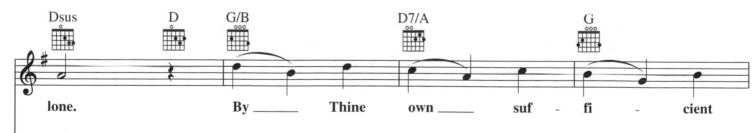

DON'T SAVE IT ALL FOR CHRISTMAS DAY

Words and Music by CELINE DION,
PETER ZIZZO and RIC WAKE

Slowly in 1, steadily

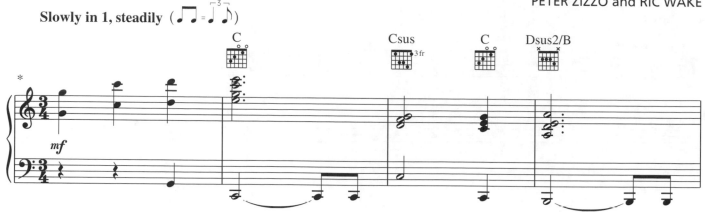

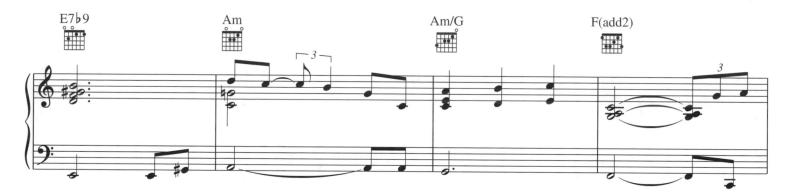

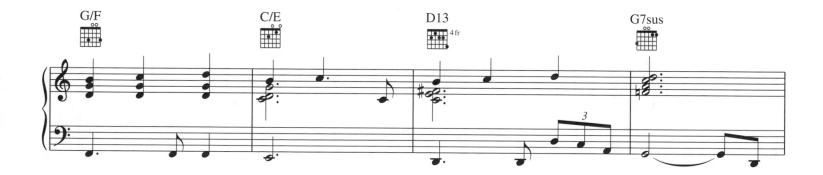

Don't get so bus-y that you miss

* Key of recording: Db

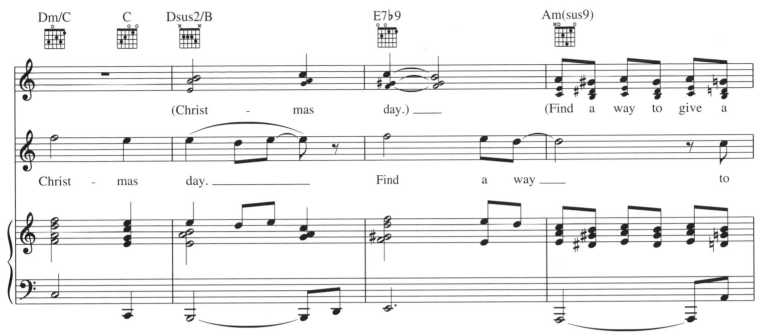

EMMANUEL

Words and Music by
MICHAEL W. SMITH

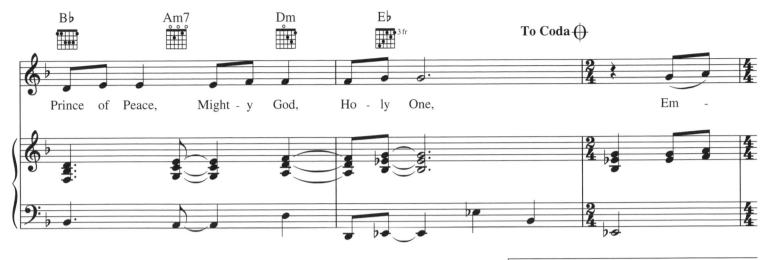

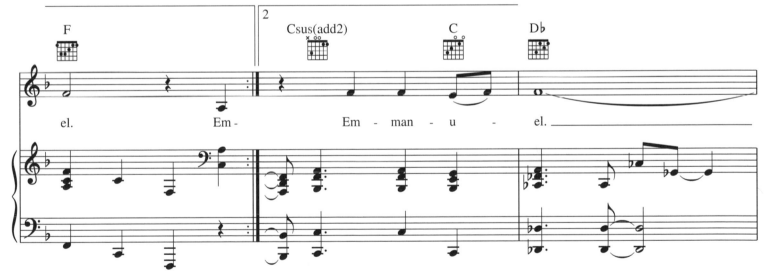

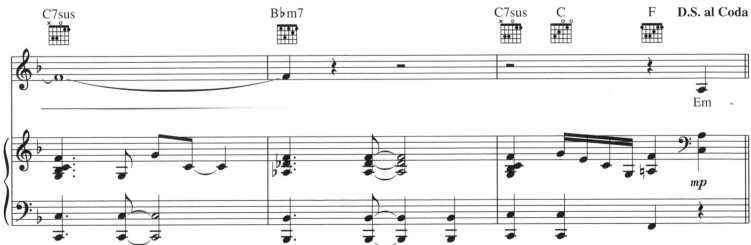

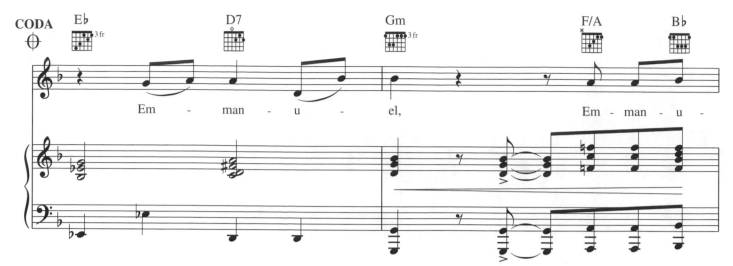

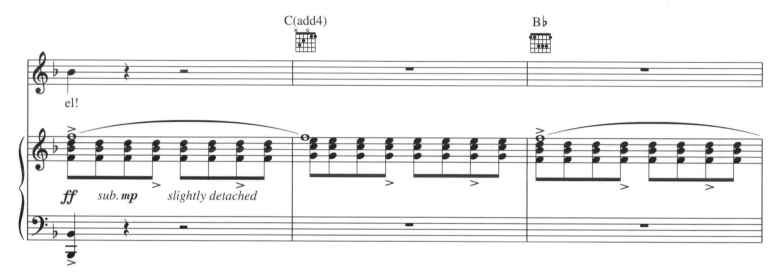

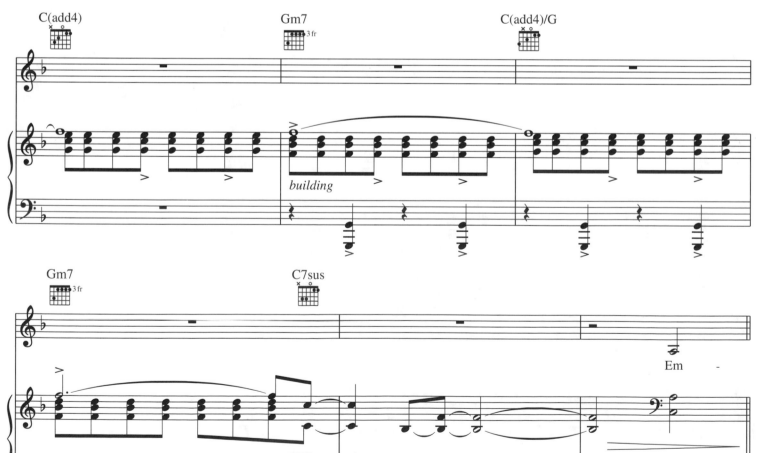

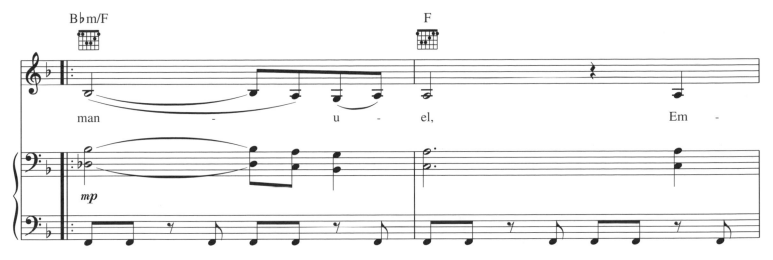

man - u - el, Em -

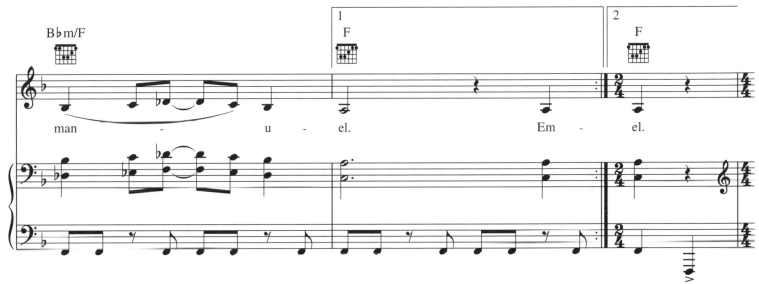

man - u - el. Em - el.

Won-der-ful Coun-sel - or, ___ Lord of life, Lord of all, ___

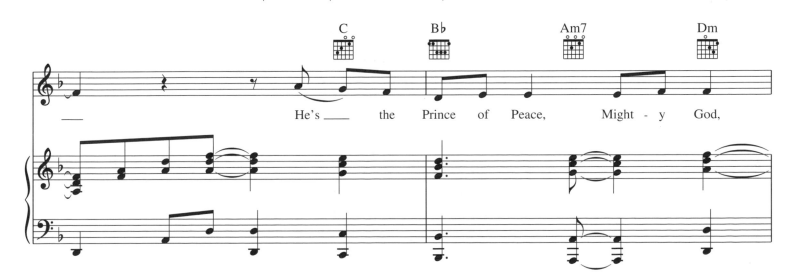

He's ___ the Prince of Peace, Might - y God,

Ho - ly One,   Em - man - u -

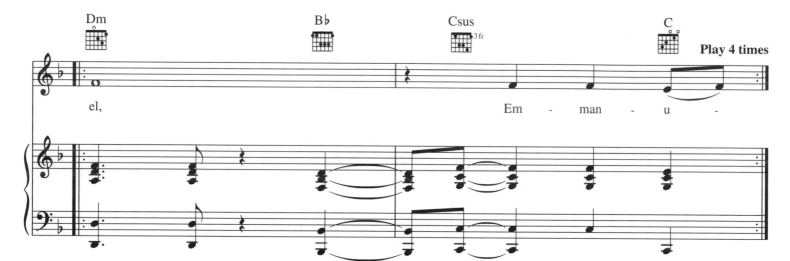

el,   Em - man - u -

Play 4 times

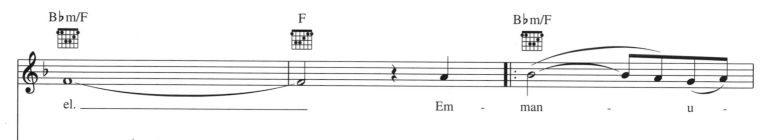

el. _____   Em - man - u -

el,   Em - man - u - el.

Play 3 times

slight rit.

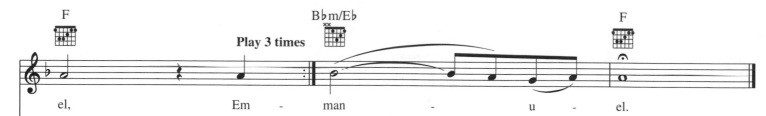

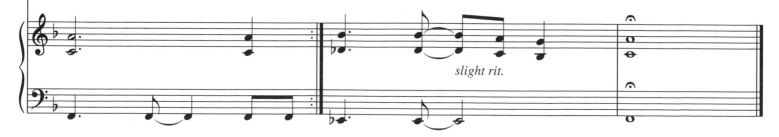

EMMANUEL, GOD WITH US

Words and Music by AMY GRANT,
CHRIS EATON and ROBERT MARSHALL

115

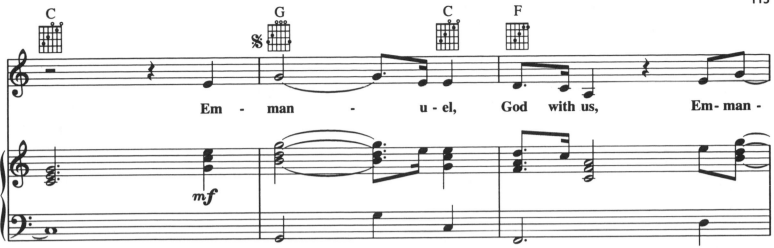

Em - man - u - el, God with us, Em- man -

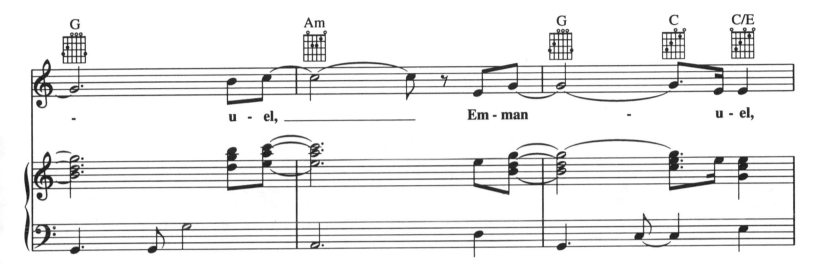

- u - el, _____ Em - man - u - el,

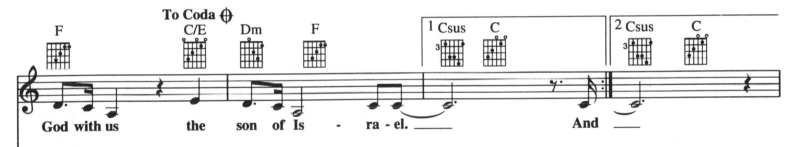

To Coda ⊕

God with us the son of Is - ra - el. _____ And ___

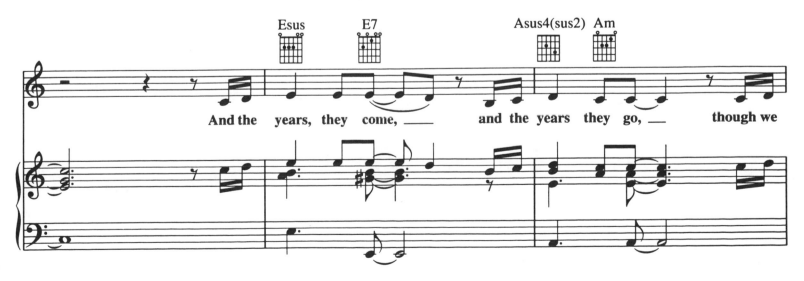

And the years, they come, ___ and the years they go, ___ though we

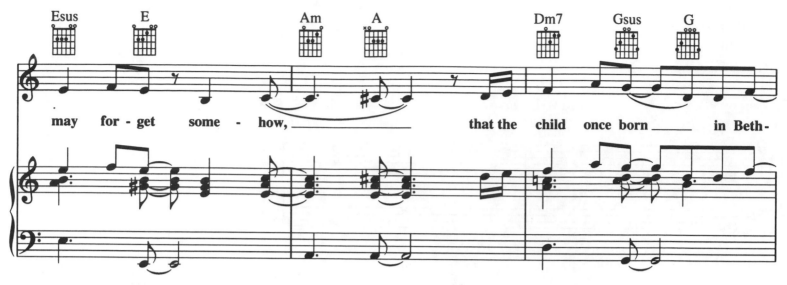

may for - get some - how, _____ that the child once born _____ in Beth-

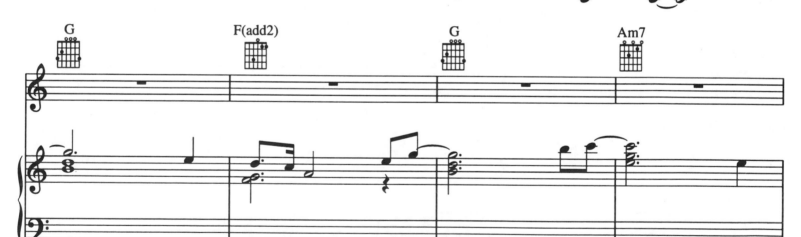

- le - hem ___ is still ___ a - mong _ us now. ___

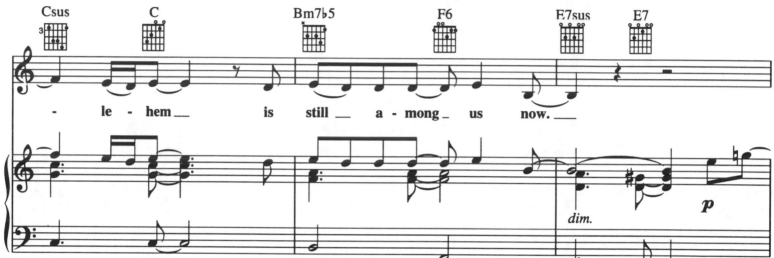

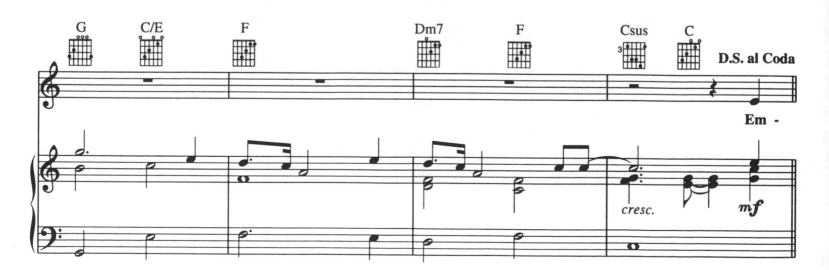

D.S. al Coda

Em -

FIRST DAY OF THE SON

Words and Music by
DERRICK PROCELL

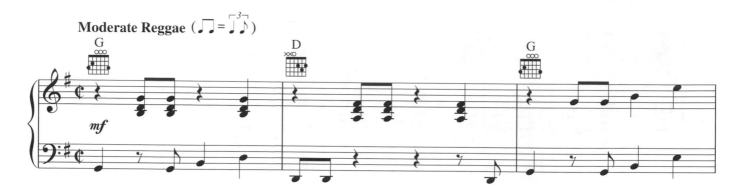

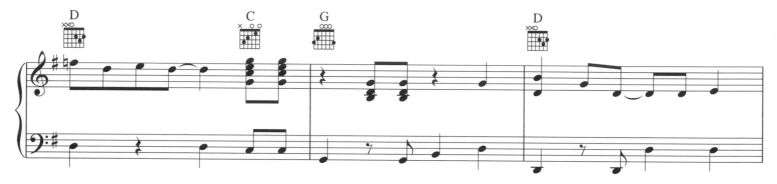

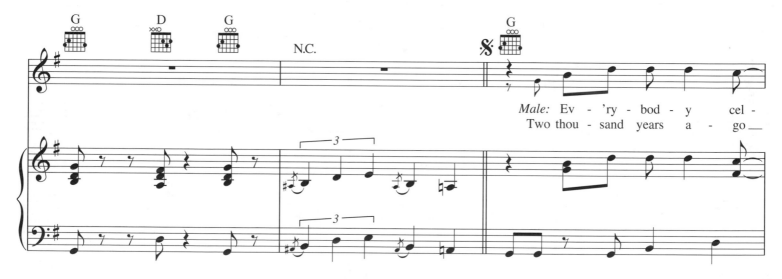

Male: Ev - 'ry - bod - y cel -
Two thou - sand years a - go ___

\- e - brate Christ - mas all a - round the world. ___
___ in a man - ger the ba - by Christ was born. ___

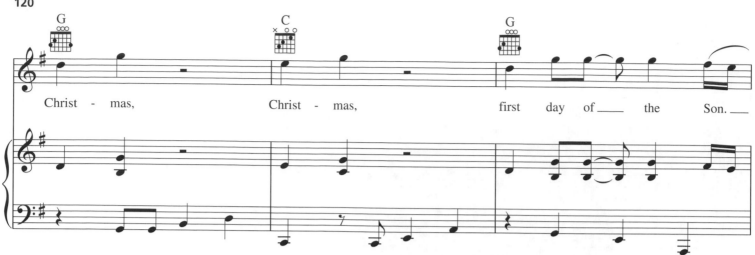

Christ - mas, Christ - mas, first day of ___ the Son. ___

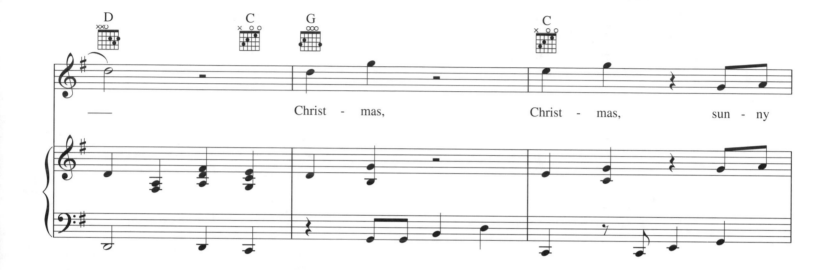

___ Christ - mas, Christ - mas, sun - ny

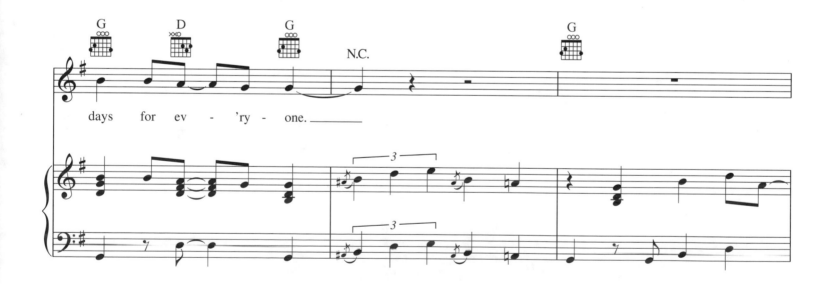

days for ev - 'ry - one. ___

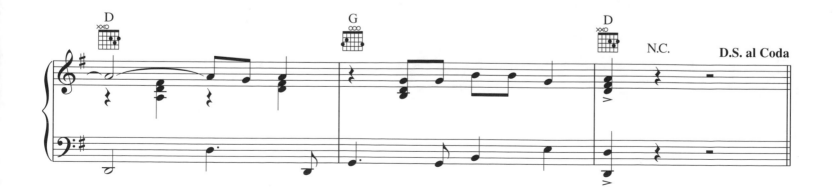

D.S. al Coda

CODA

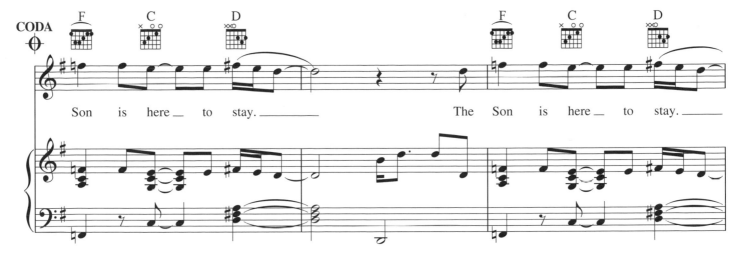

Son is here __ to stay. _____ The Son is here __ to stay. _____

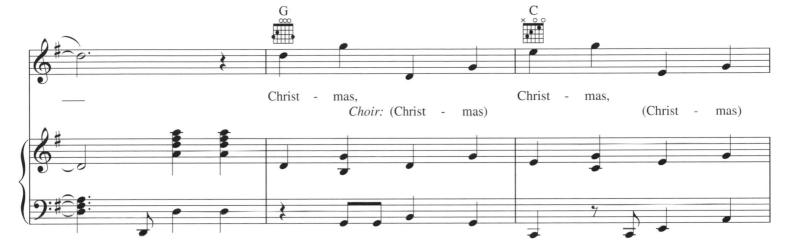

_____ Christ - mas, Christ - mas, (Christ - mas)

Choir: (Christ - mas)

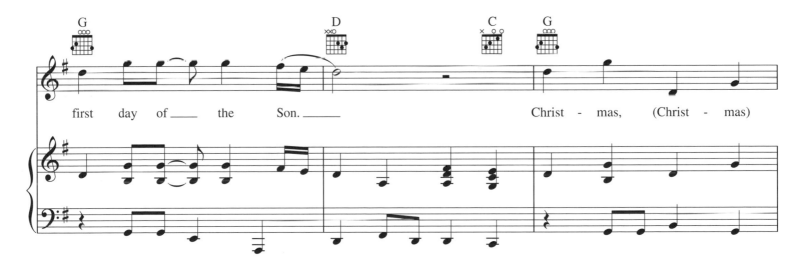

first day of ___ the Son. _____ Christ - mas, (Christ - mas)

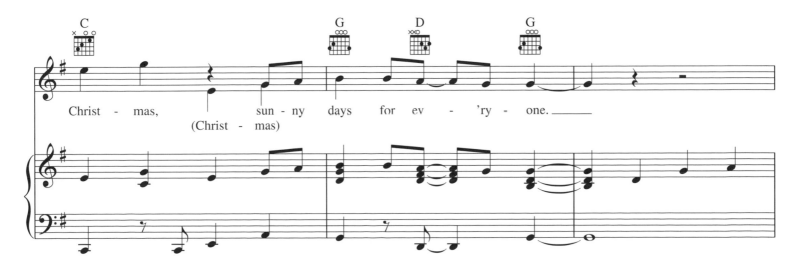

Christ - mas, sun - ny days for ev - 'ry - one. _____

(Christ - mas)

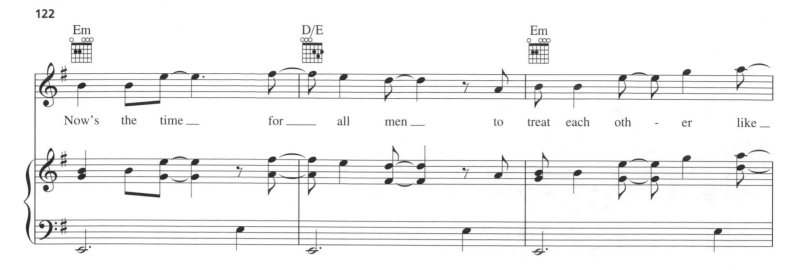

Now's the time ___ for ___ all men ___ to treat each oth - er like ___

___ good friends. ___ Peace on earth, mer - cy too! ___

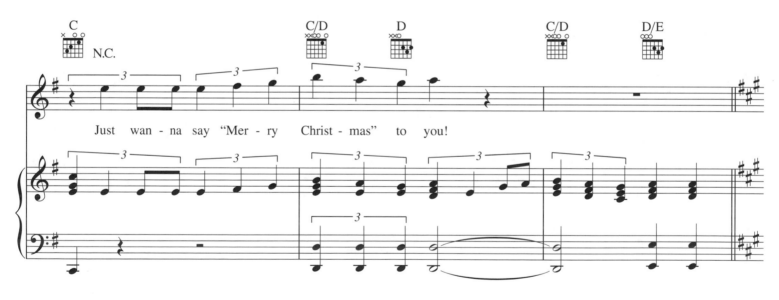

Just wan - na say "Mer - ry Christ - mas" to you!

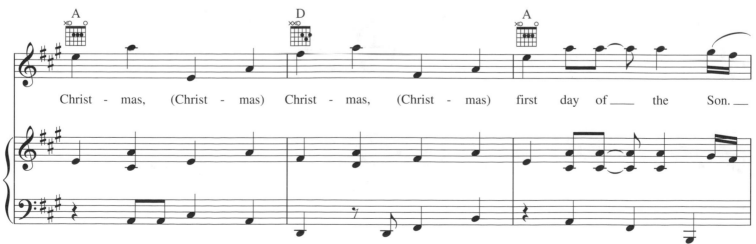

Christ - mas, (Christ - mas) Christ - mas, (Christ - mas) first day of ___ the Son. ___

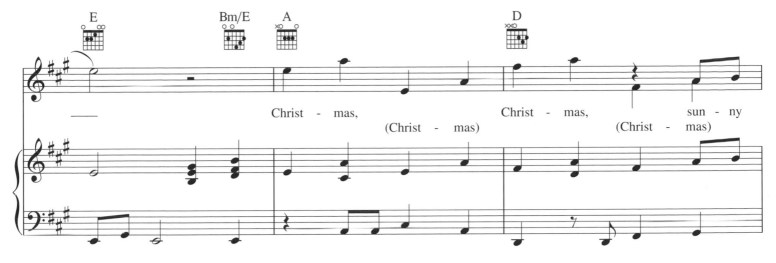

Christ - mas, Christ - mas, sun - ny
(Christ - mas) (Christ - mas)

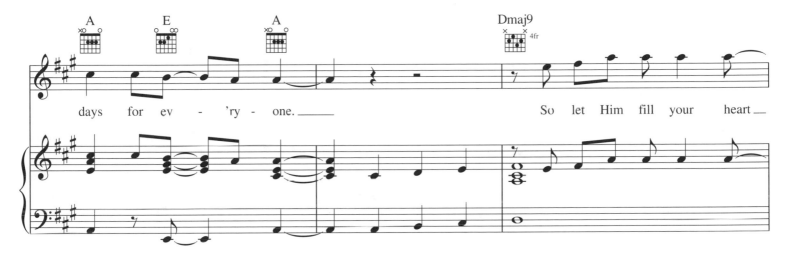

days for ev - 'ry - one. _____ So let Him fill your heart _____

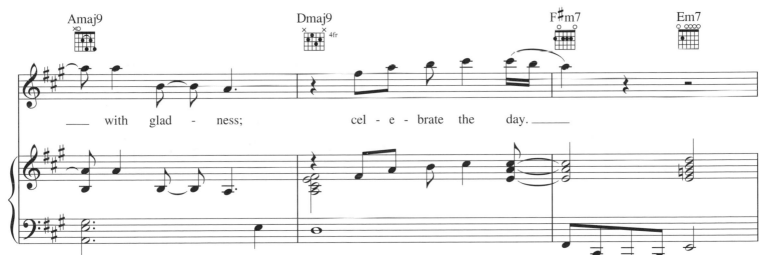

_____ with glad - ness; cel - e - brate the day. _____

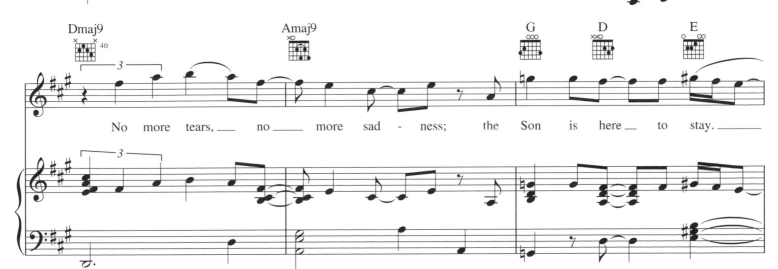

No more tears, _____ no _____ more sad - ness; the Son is here _____ to stay. _____

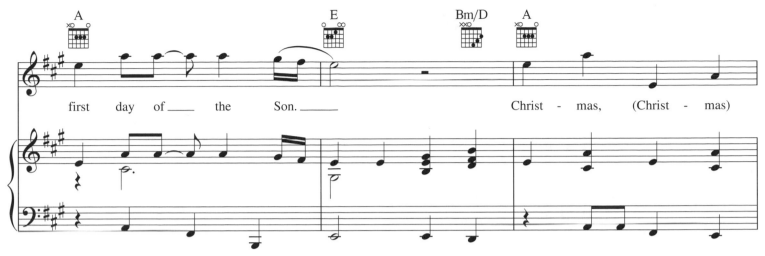

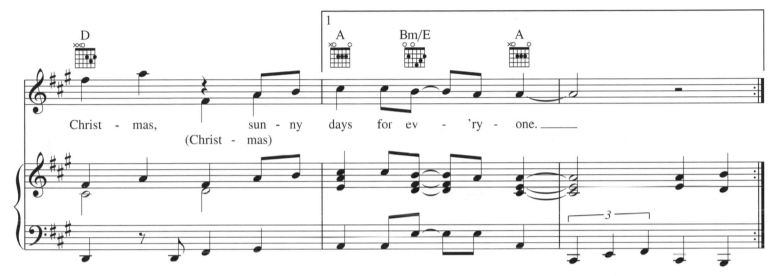

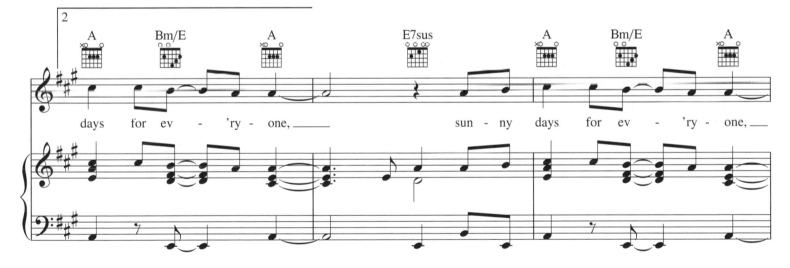

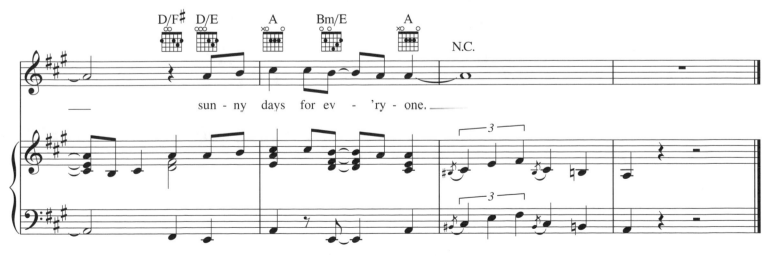

GLORIA

Words and Music by MICHAEL W. SMITH
Based on "Angels We Have Heard On High"

Very rhythmic ♩=108

An – gels we have heard on high,

Sweet – ly sing – ing o'er the plains,

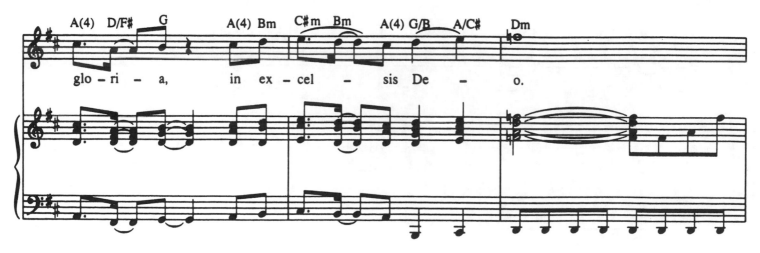

(Glo – ri – a, oh, sing glo – ri – a.) Him whose birth the

an – gels sing;___ (Glo – ri – a, oh, sing glo – ri – a.)

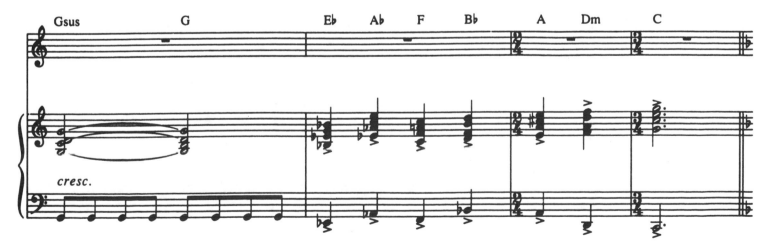

IMMANUEL

Words and Music by
MICHAEL CARD

1. A sign shall be giv-en, a vir-gin will con-
(2.) What shall be your an-swer? Oh, will you hear the

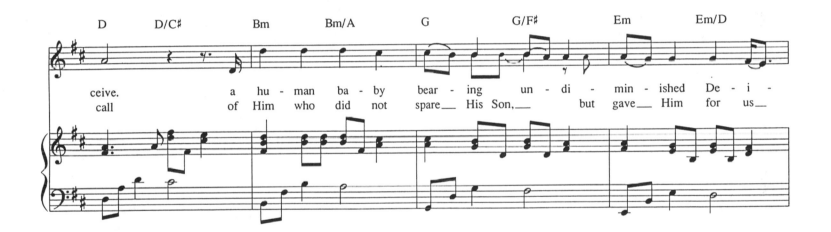

ceive. a hu-man ba-by bear-ing un-di-min-ished De-i-
call of Him who did not spare His Son, but gave Him for us

ty. The glo-ry of the na-tions, a light for all to
all? On earth there is no pow-er, there is no depth or

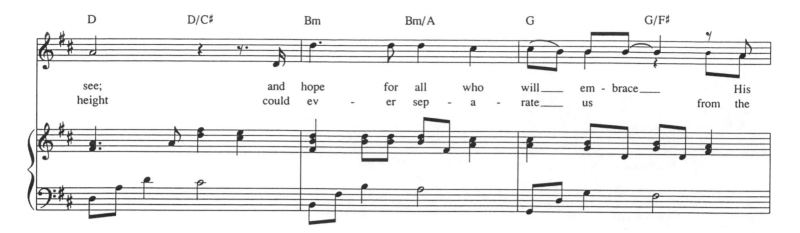

see;
height

and hope for all who will___ em-brace___ His
could ev - er sep - a - rate___ us from the

warm re - al - i - ty.
love of God in___ Christ. }

Im - man - u -

(Chorus - last time: f)

el,
(3rd time: is with___

Our God is with___ us.
us.

And___ if
___ If)

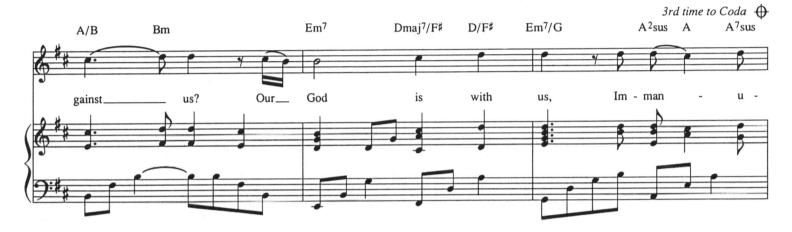

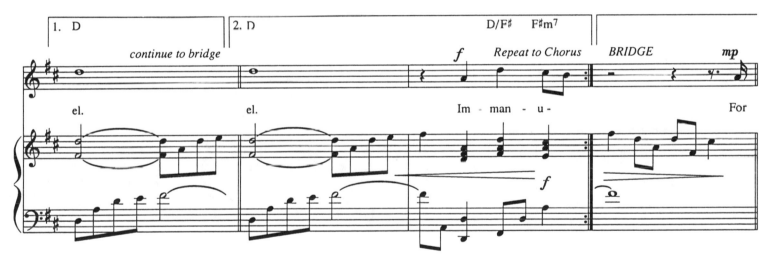

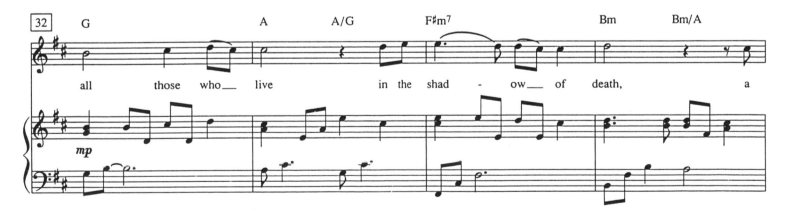

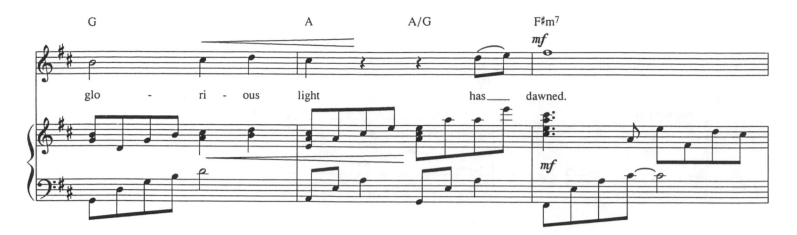

glo - ri - ous light has dawned.

For all those who stum - ble in the

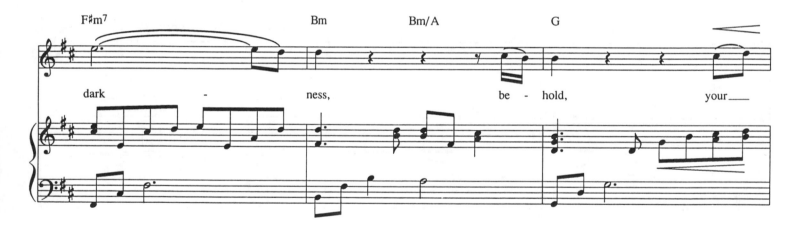

dark - ness, be - hold, your

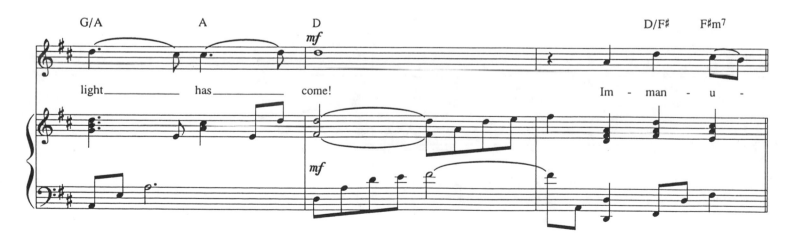

light has come! Im - man - u -

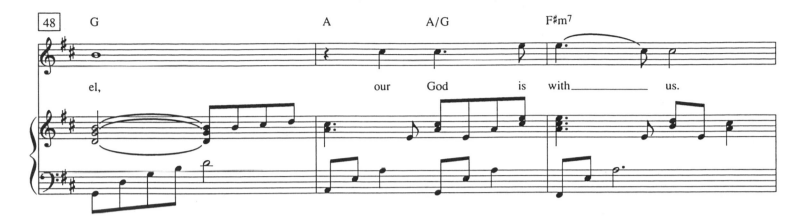

el,   our God   is with_____ us.

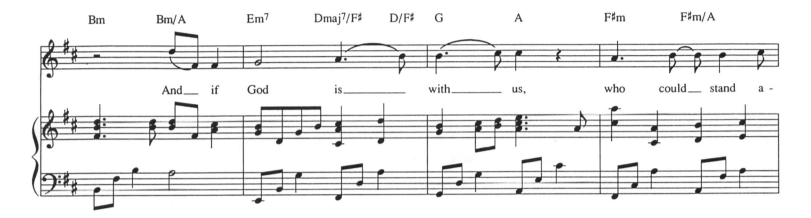

And__ if God   is_____ with_____ us,   who could__ stand a-

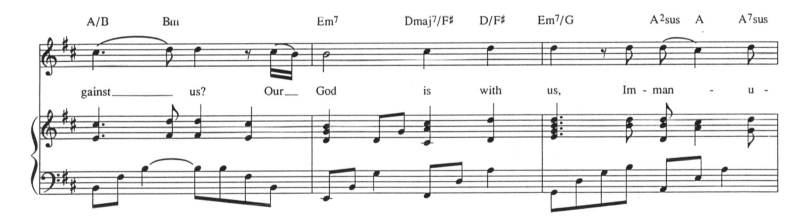

gainst_____ us?   Our__ God   is   with us,   Im - man - u -

D.S. al Coda 𝄋 ⨁ *CODA*

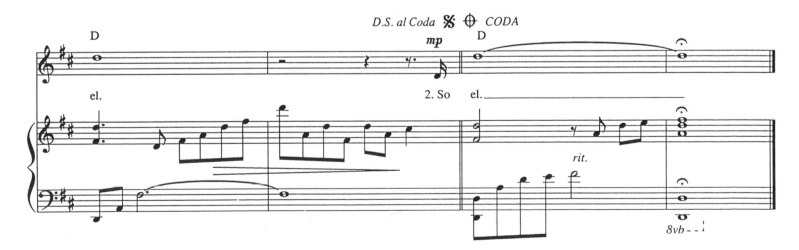

el.   2. So el._____

IT'S THE THOUGHT

Words and Music by
TWILA PARIS

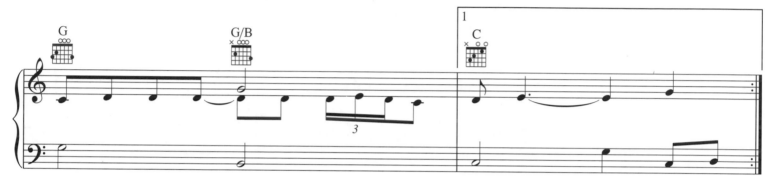

And a lov - ing
lov - ing

thought   sends us   out   to   find   some - thing
thought   sent   a   snow white Lamb   to   a

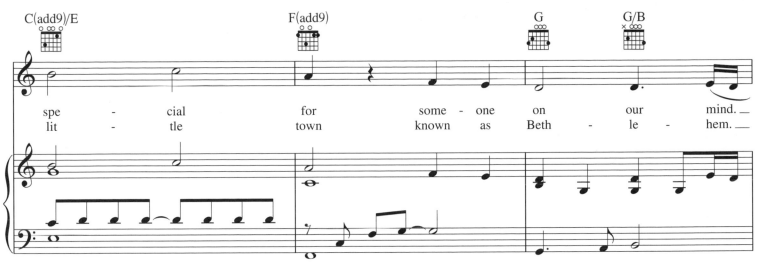

spe - cial for some - one on our mind.
lit - tle for town known as Beth - le - hem.

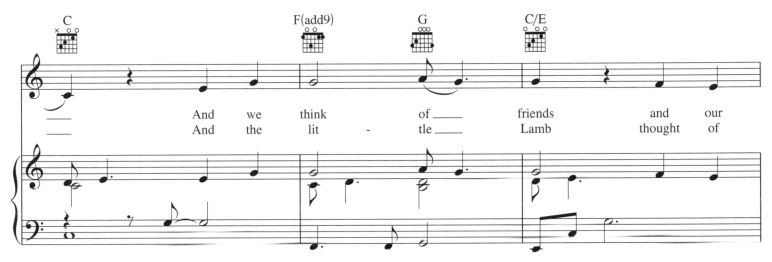

And we think of ____ friends and our
And the lit - tle ____ Lamb thought of

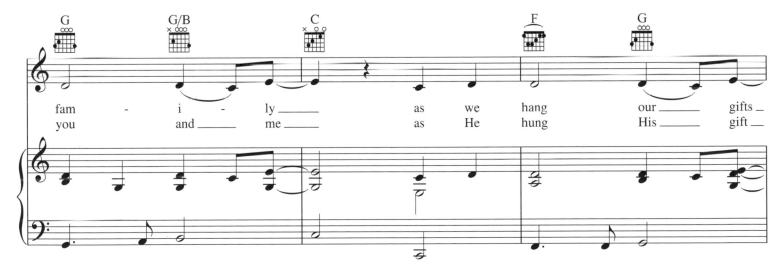

fam - i - ly ____ as we hang our ____ gifts
you and ____ me ____ as He hung His ____ gift

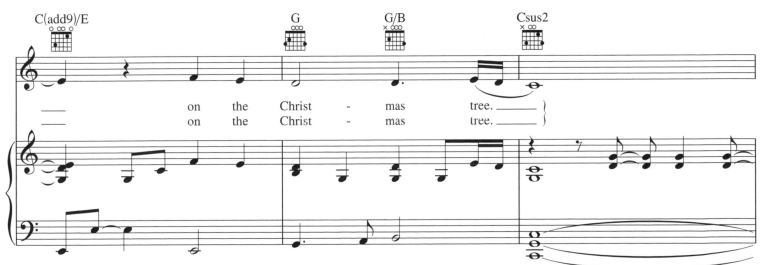

____ on the Christ - mas tree. ____
____ on the Christ - mas tree. ____

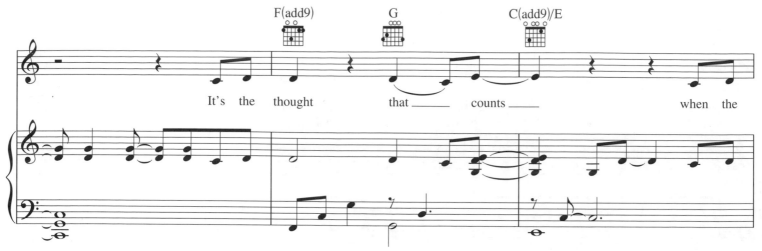

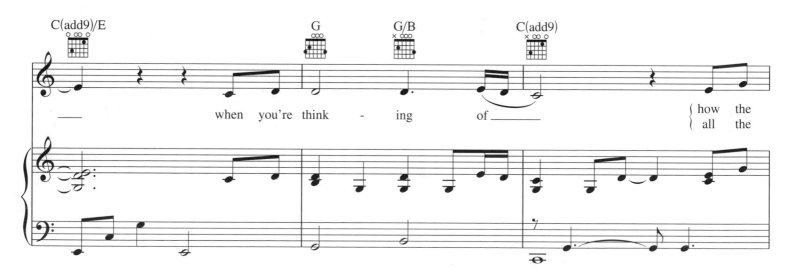

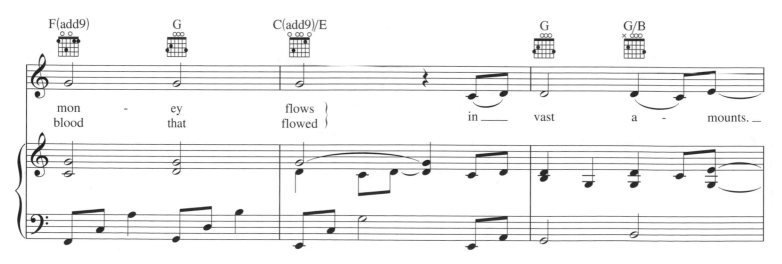

When the thought is _____ love, _____ it's the

thought that _____ counts. _____

And a _____

Think of _____ the pre - cious _____ gift He

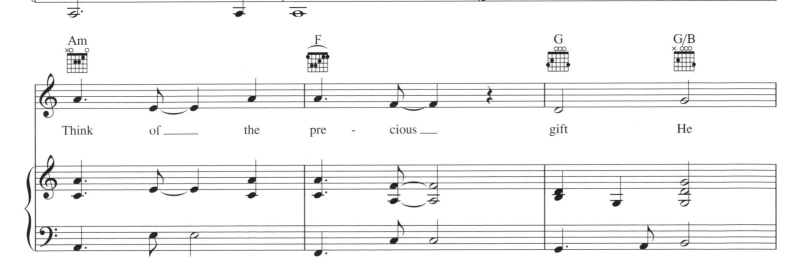

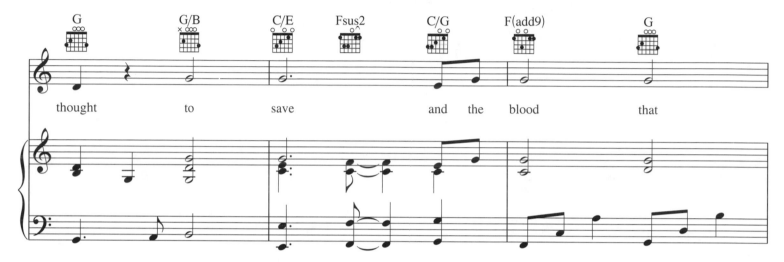

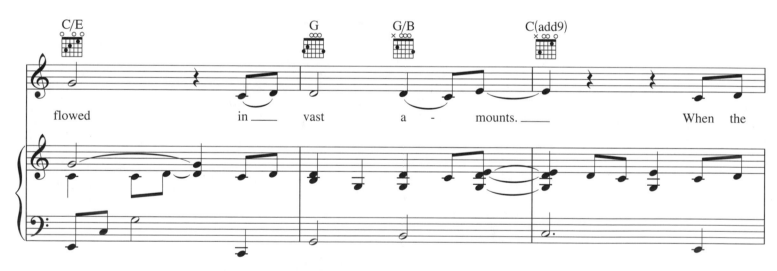

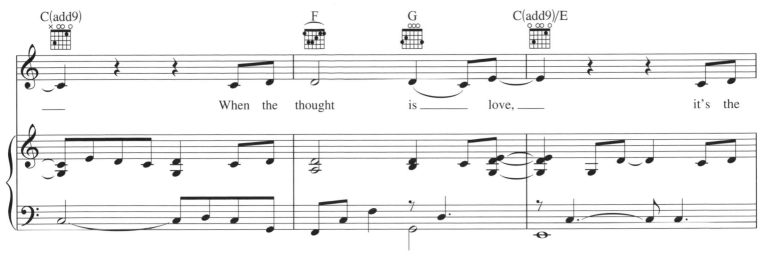

When the thought is _____ love, _____ it's the

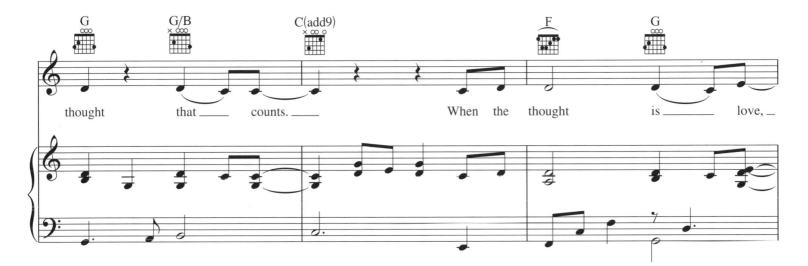

thought that _____ counts. _____ When the thought is _____ love, __

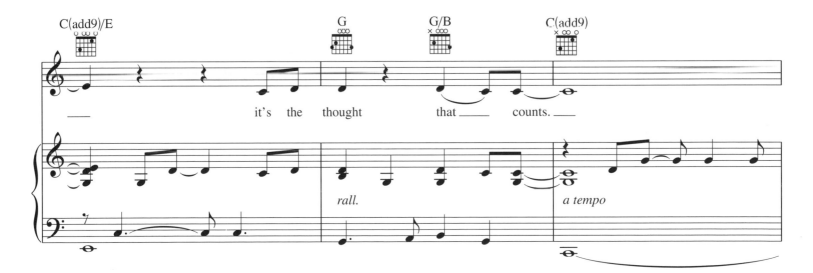

it's the thought that _____ counts. _____

JESUS BORN ON THIS DAY

Words and Music by MARIAH CAREY
and WALTER AFANASIEFF

Moderately slow

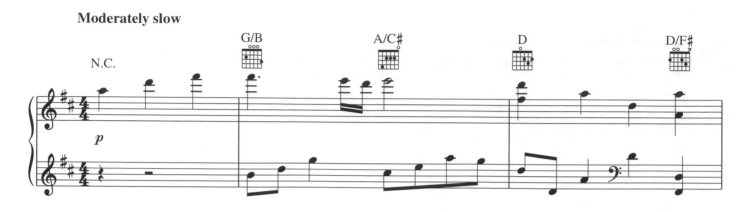

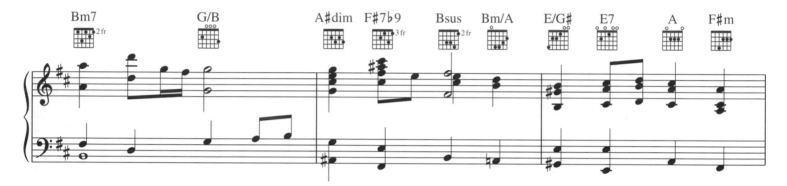

Slower

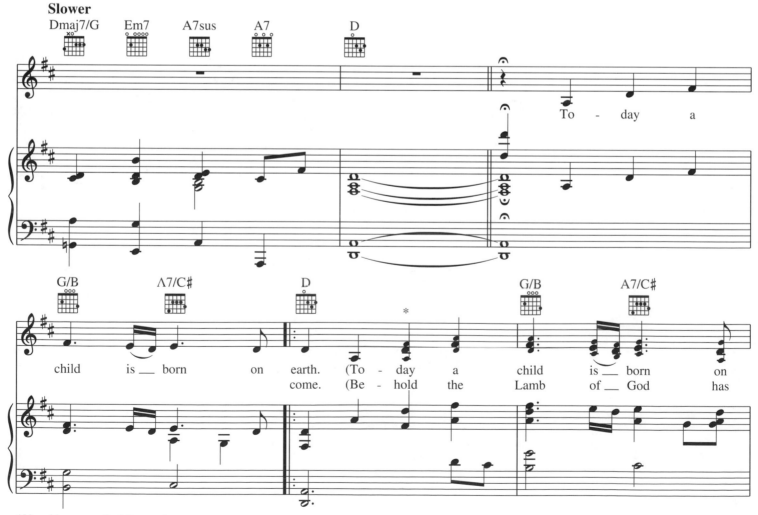

child is __ born on earth. (To - day a child is __ born on
come. (Be - hold the Lamb of __ God has

*Vocal harmony 2nd time only

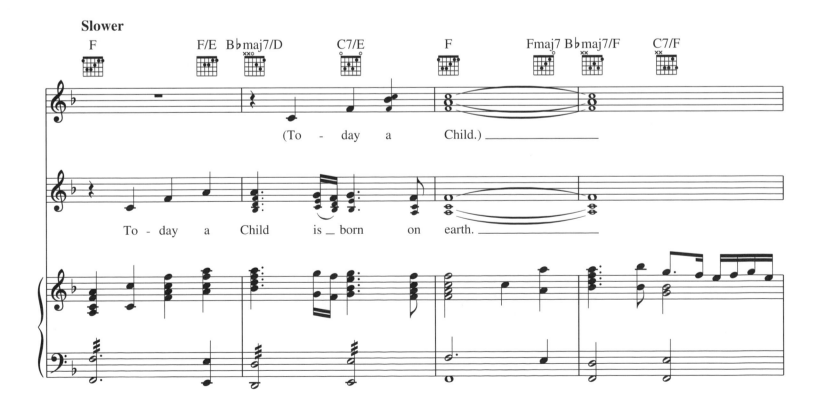

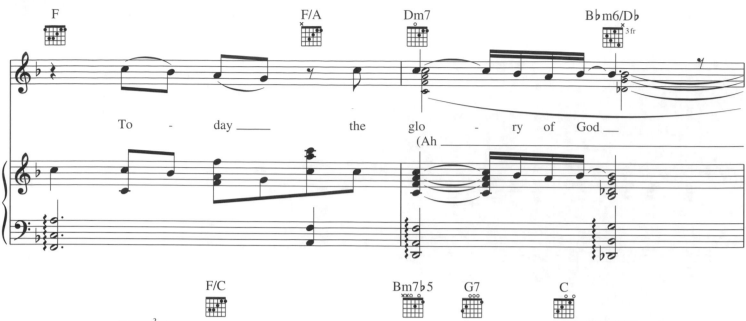

To - day _____ the glo - ry of God _____
(Ah _____

shines ev - 'ry - where _____ for all of the world. _____
ah _____)

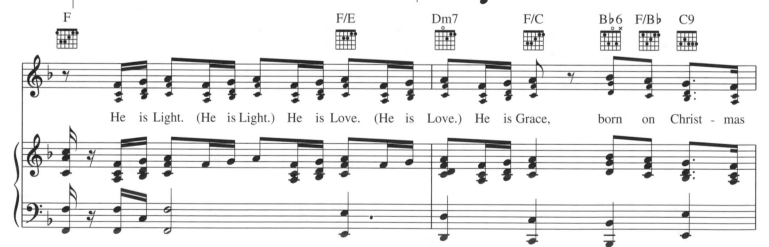

He is Light. (He is Light.) He is Love. (He is Love.) He is Grace, born on Christ - mas

day. He is Light. (He is Light.) He is Love. (He is Love.) He is Grace, born on Christ - mas

JOSEPH'S SONG

Words and Music by
MICHAEL CARD

the an - gel said.
this ba - by be.
it shines a - gain.

How could it be?
the son of my
How could it

4th time to Coda

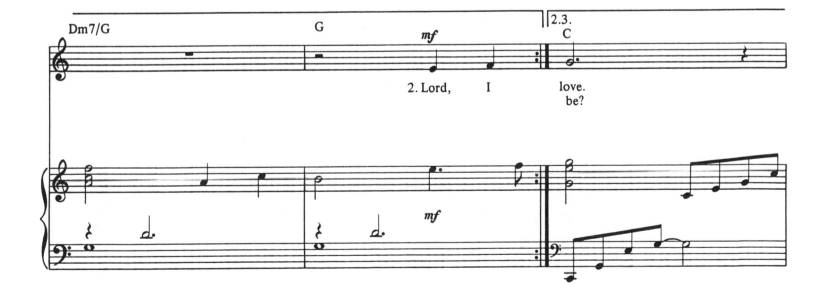

2. Lord, I love.
be?

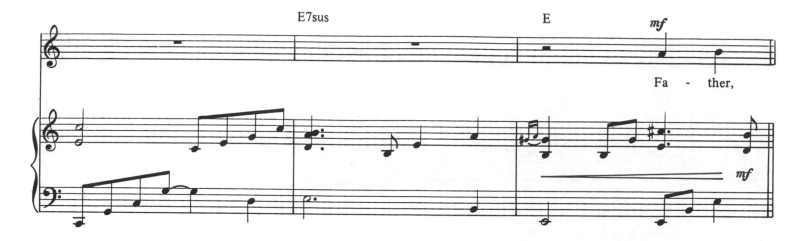

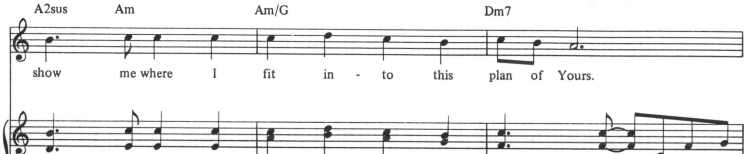

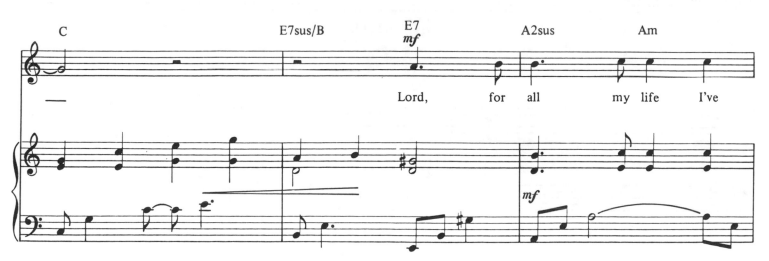

been a sim-ple car-pen-ter. How

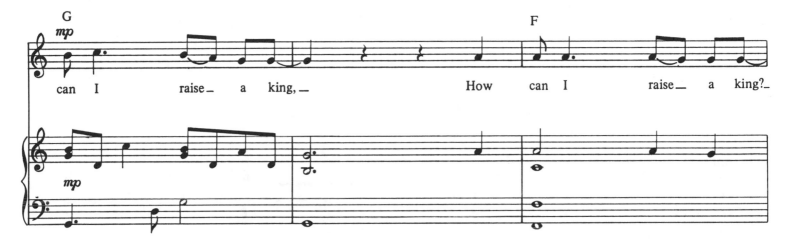

can I raise a king, — How can I raise a king?

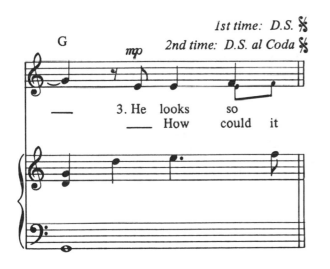

1st time: D.S. %
2nd time: D.S. al Coda %

— 3. He looks so
— How could it

Coda

be?

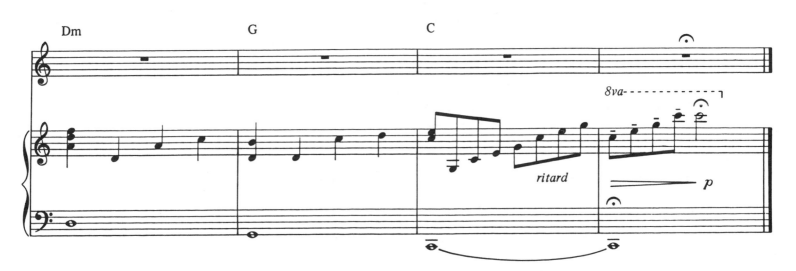

JOY
(To the World)

Words and Music by DAN MUCKALA,
GRANT CUNNINGHAM and BROWN BANNISTER

D.S. al Coda

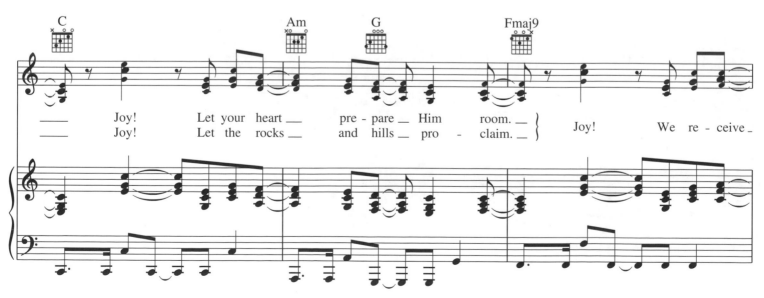

LIGHT A CANDLE

Words and Music by JOEL LINDSAY
and WAYNE HAUN

LITTLE TOWN

Words and Music by
CHRIS EATON

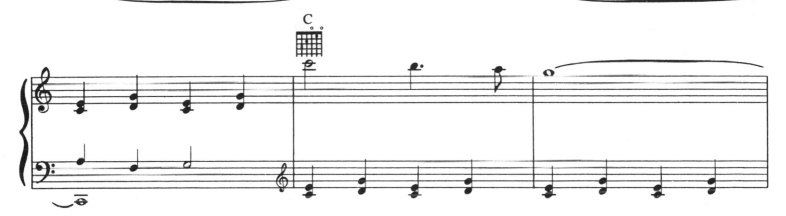

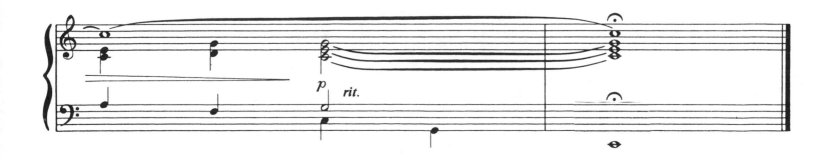

LOVE HAS COME

Words and Music by AMY GRANT,
SHANE KEISTER and MICHAEL W. SMITH

Hur - ry now, wake up your eyes, time for lit - tle ones to see;
I could have a spe - cial dream com - ing true on Christ - mas morn,

Dad - dy's got a big sur - prise hid - ing there be - neath the Christ - mas tree.
I would want the world to see how His Fa - ther smiled when Christ was born,

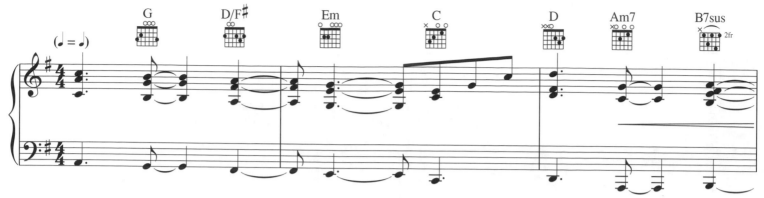

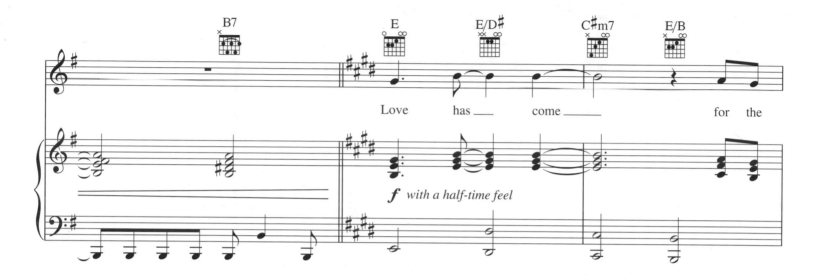

Love has ___ come ___ for the

world to ___ know, ___ as the wise men ___ knew ___

___ such a long time ___ a-go. ___ And I be-lieve that

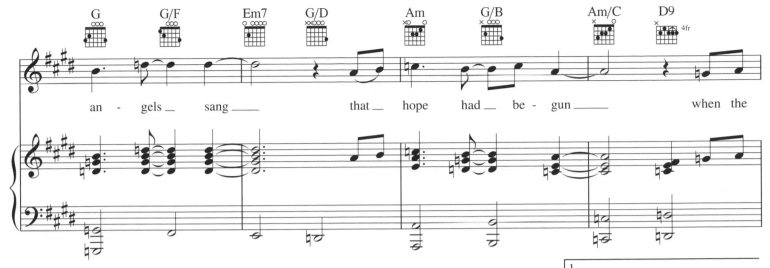

an - gels __ sang __ that __ hope had __ be - gun __ when the

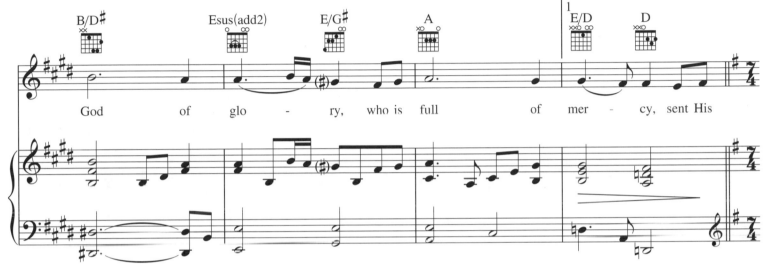

God of glo - ry, who is full of mer - cy, sent His

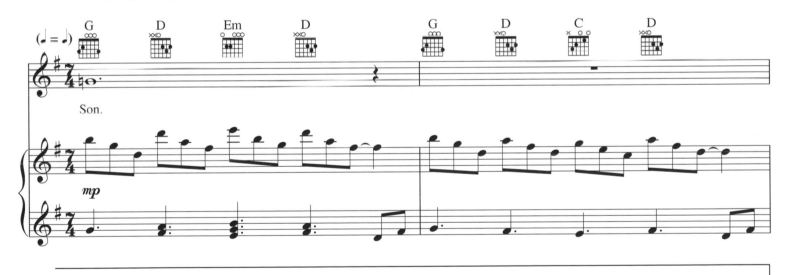

Son.

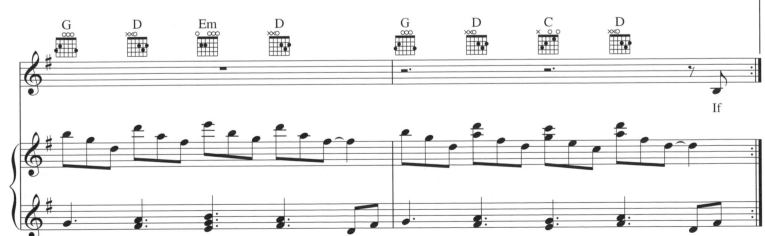

If

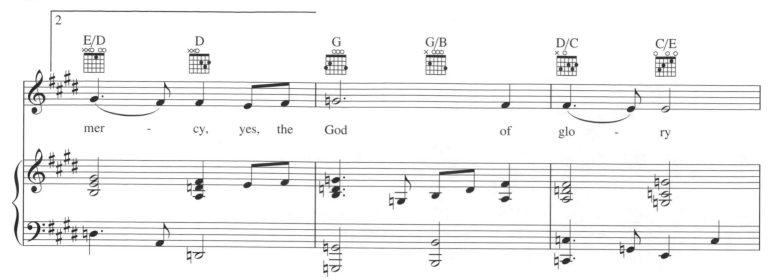

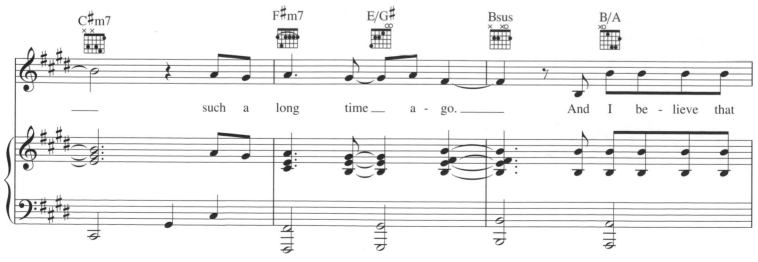

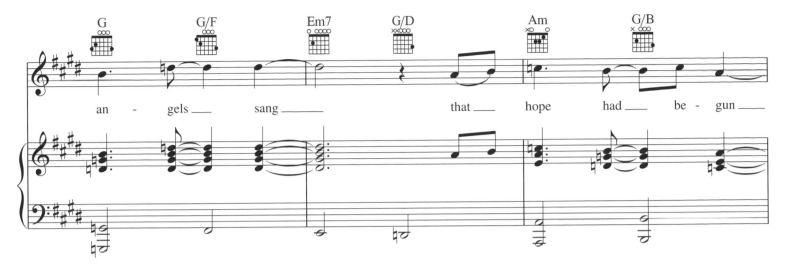

an - gels sang that hope had be - gun

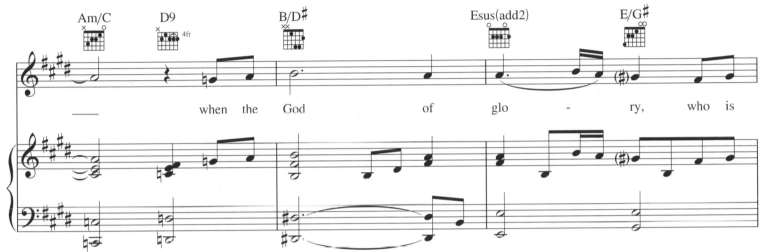

when the God of glo - ry, who is

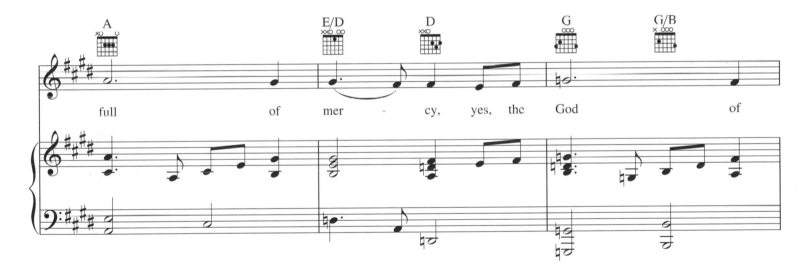

full of mer - cy, yes, the God of

Repeat and Fade | **Optional Ending**

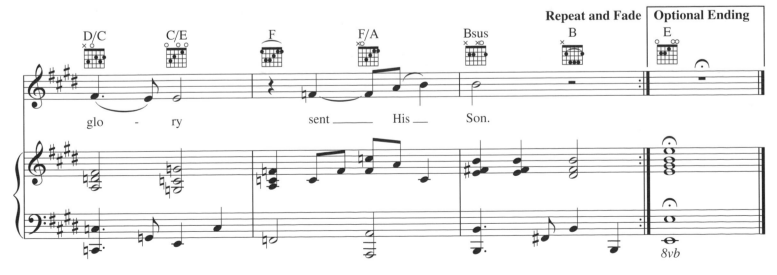

glo - ry sent His Son.

NO EYE HAD SEEN

Words by AMY GRANT
Music by MICHAEL W. SMITH

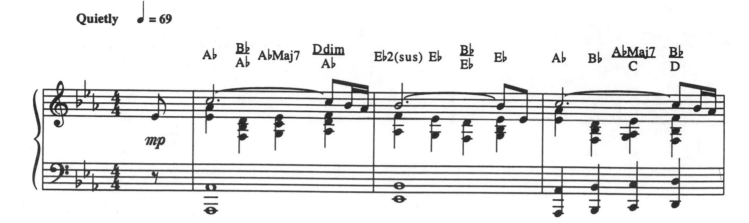

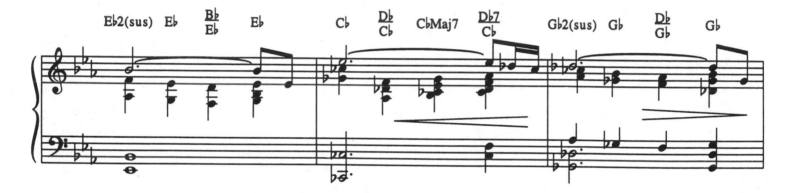

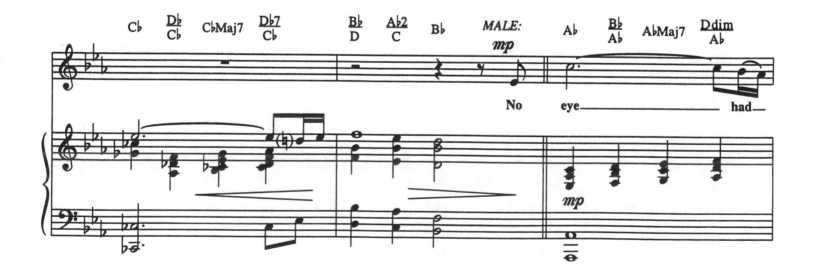

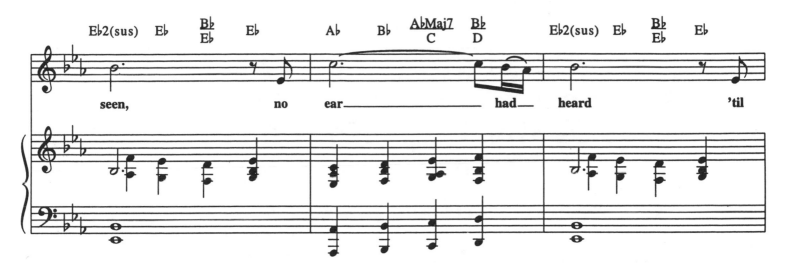

seen, no ear_____ had__ heard 'til

hosts_____ on__ high pro - claimed_____ the__

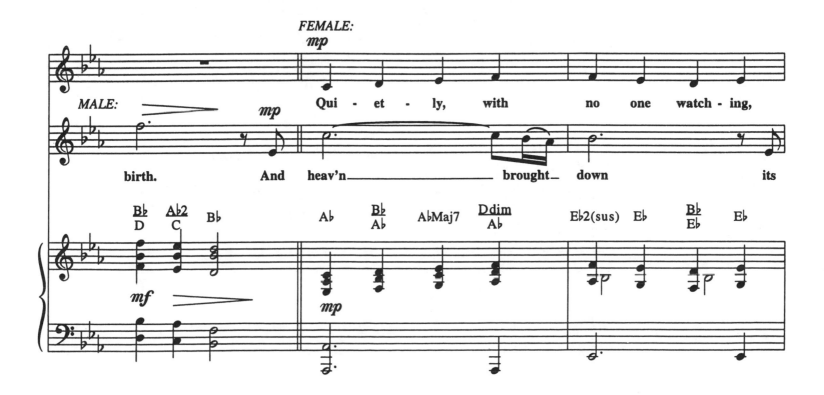

MALE: birth. And heav'n_____ brought__ down its

FEMALE: Qui - et - ly, with no one watch - ing,

from the womb of per-fect peace, Well- spring of the
on - ly— Child, the Son——— of—

joy de-liv-ered in - to earth-ly des-ti-ny.
man the world rec-on-ciled.

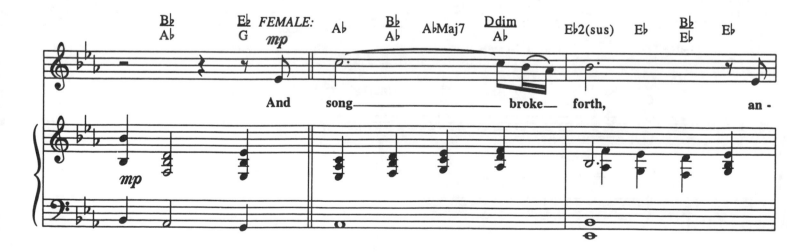

FEMALE:

And song——— broke— forth, an-

NOT THAT FAR FROM BETHLEHEM

Words and Music by JEFF BORDERS,
GAYLA BORDERS and LOWELL ALEXANDER

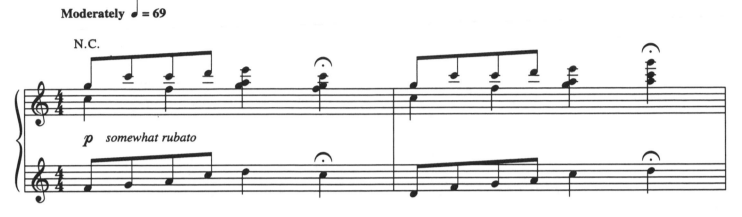

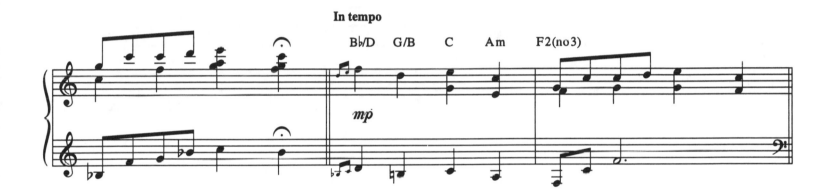

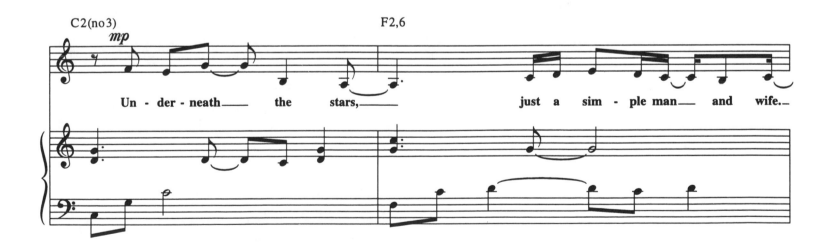

Un - der - neath the stars, just a sim - ple man and wife.

Some - where in the dark his words cut the si - lent night:

"Take my hand, for the Child that you car - ry is God's

own. And though it seems the road is long, we're

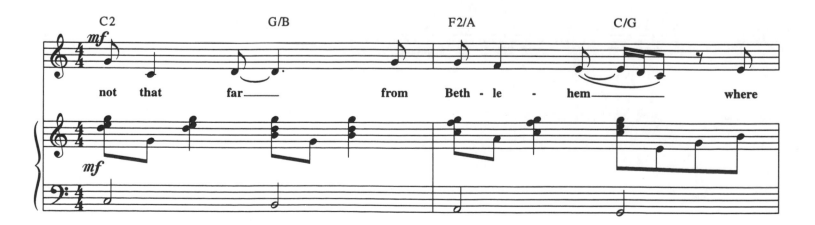

not that far from Beth - le - hem where

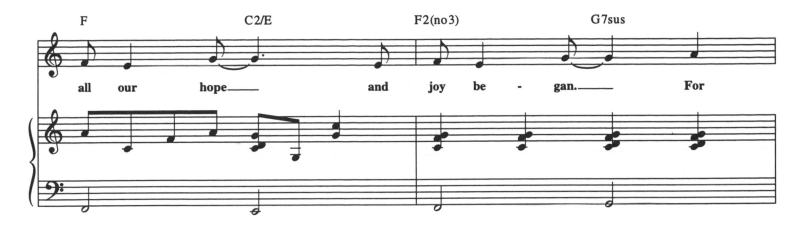

all our hope____ and joy be - gan.____ For

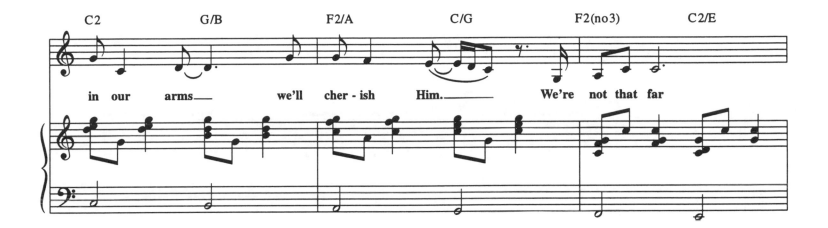

in our arms____ we'll cher - ish Him._____ We're not that far

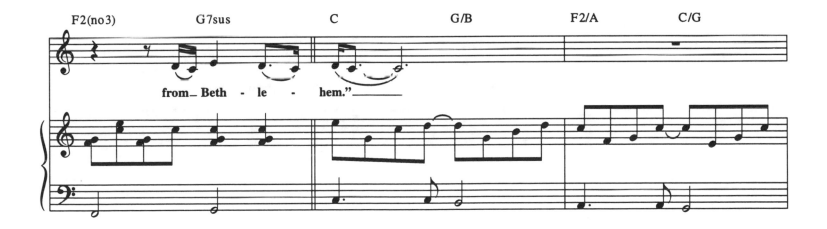

from__ Beth - le - hem."_____

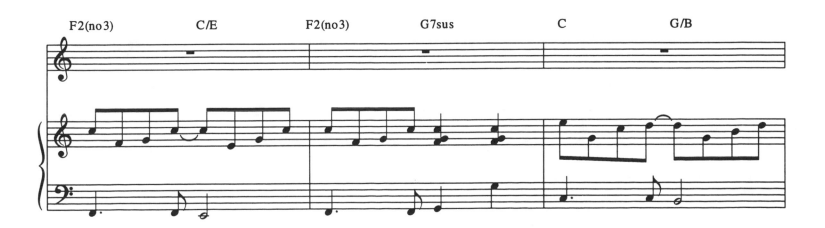

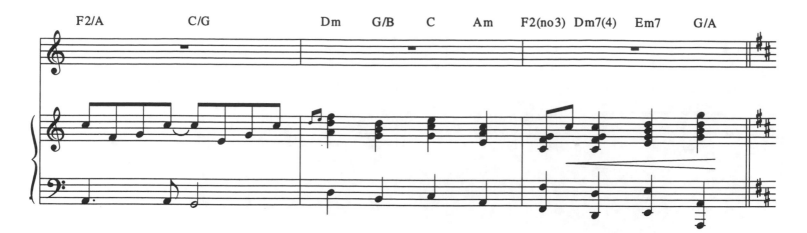

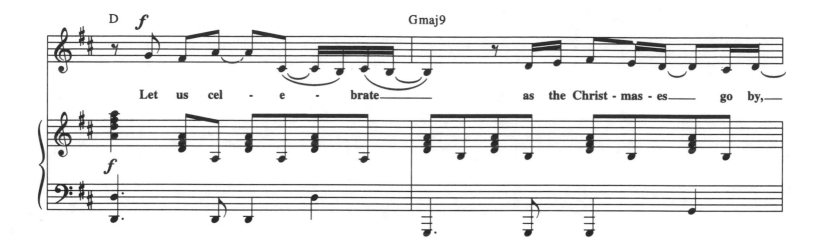

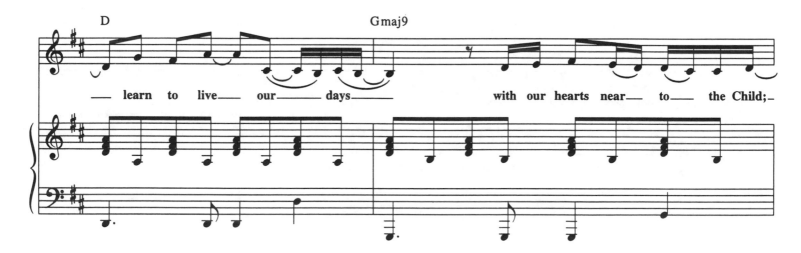

lasts.＿ And though two thou - sand＿ years＿ have passed,＿

we're＿ not that far＿ from

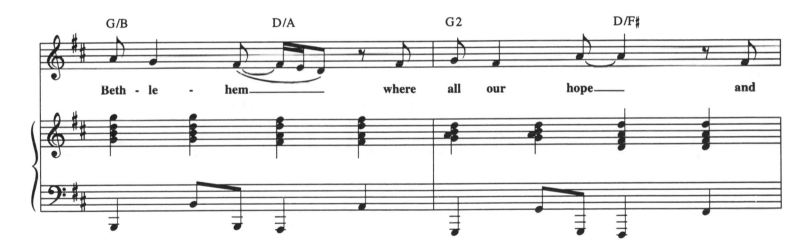

Beth - le - hem＿ where all our hope＿ and

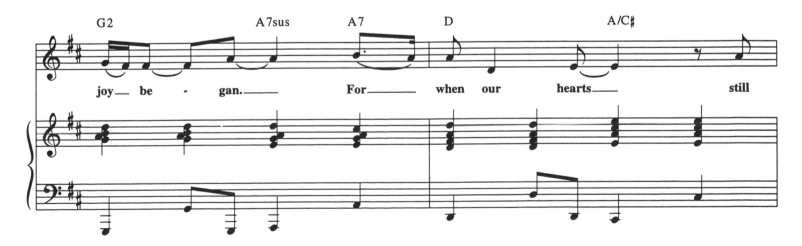

joy＿ be - gan.＿ For＿ when our hearts＿ still

cher - ish Him,_____ we're not that far._____

_____ We're_____ not that far_____ from

Beth - le - hem_____ _____ where all our hope_____ and

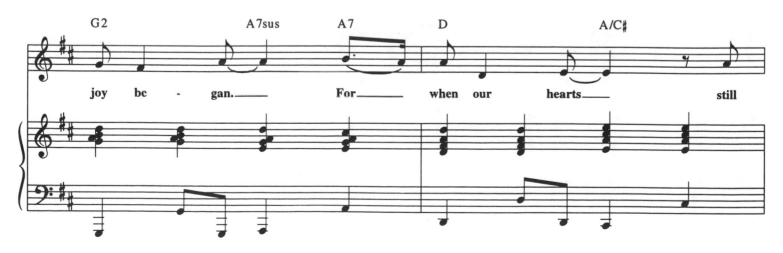

joy be - gan._____ For_____ when our hearts_____ still

cher-ish Him,___ we're not that far,___ we're

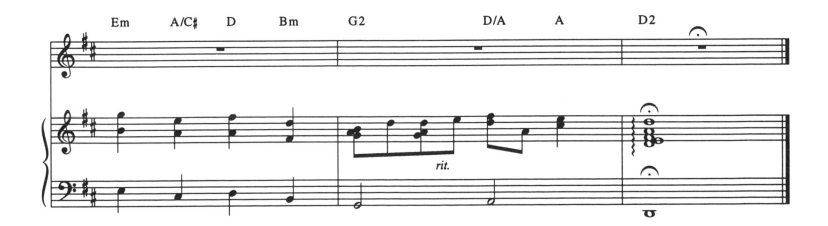

not that far___ from__ Beth - le -

hem. ___

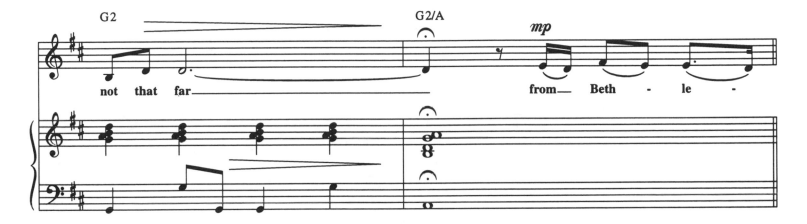

O COME, ALL YE FAITHFUL

Words and Music by REBECCA ST. JAMES
and TEDD TJORNHOM

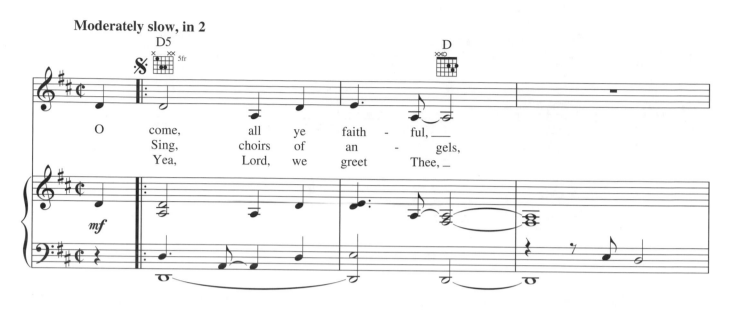

O come, all ye faith - ful, ___
Sing, choirs of an - gels,
Yea, Lord, we greet Thee, ___

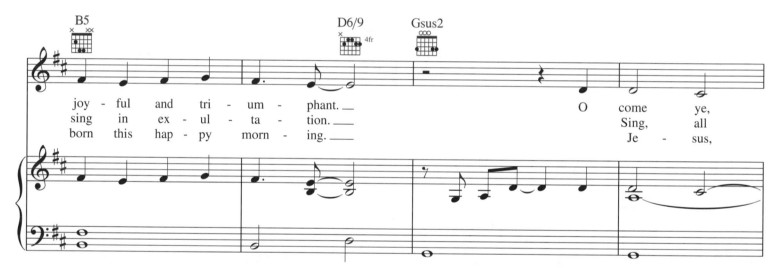

joy - ful and tri - um - phant. ___
sing in ex - ul - ta - tion. ___
born this hap - py morn - ing. ___
O come ye,
Sing, all
Je - sus,

O come ___ ye to Beth - le - hem.
ye cit - i - zens of ___ heav - en.
to Thee ___ be all ___ glo - ry.

Come and __ be -
Glo - ry __ to
Word of __ the

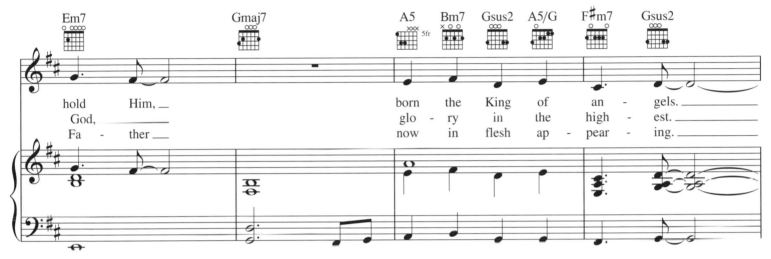

hold Him, __
God, __
Fa - ther __

born the King of an - gels. __
glo - ry in the high - est. __
now in flesh ap - pear - ing. __

O come let us a - dore Him, __ O come let us a -

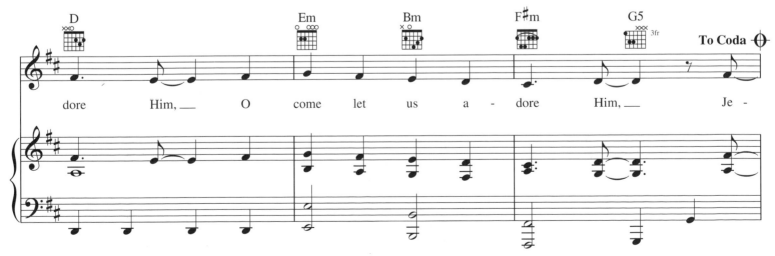

dore Him, __ O come let us a - dore Him, __ Je -

To Coda

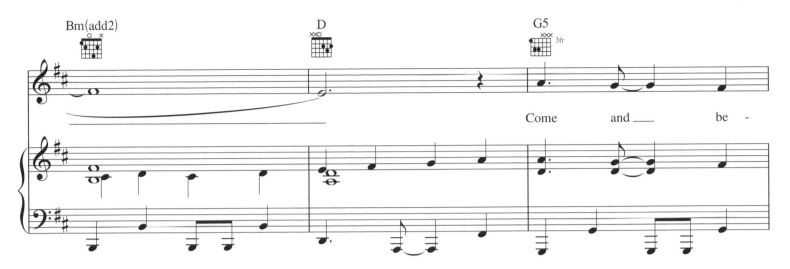

Come and ___ be-

hold Him, ___

born the King ___ of an - gels. ___

D.S. al Coda

CODA

- sus. ___

O come let us a -

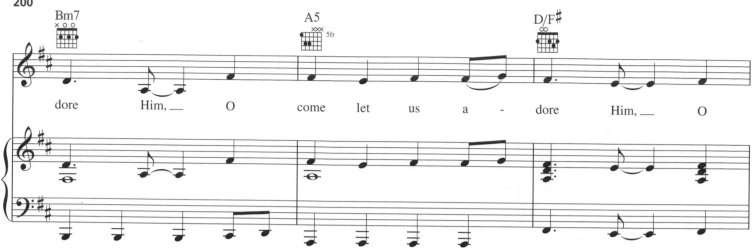

dore Him, __ O come let us a - dore Him, __ O

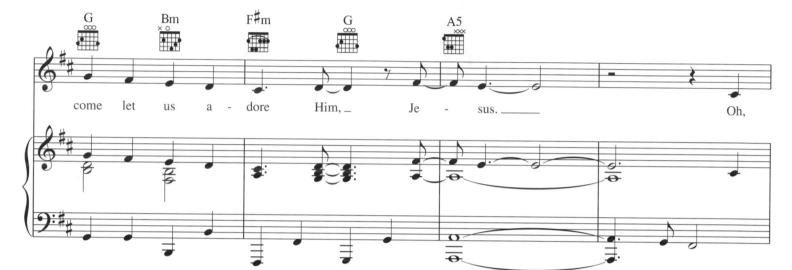

come let us a - dore Him, _ Je - sus. _____ Oh,

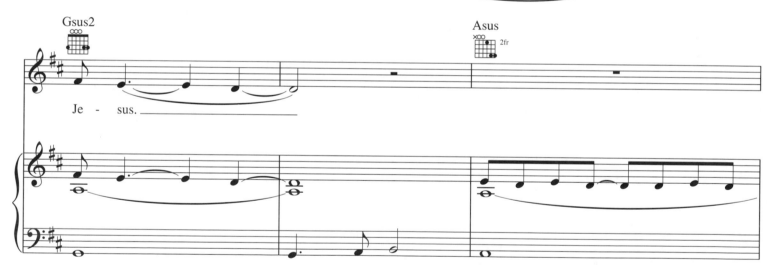

Je - sus. _____

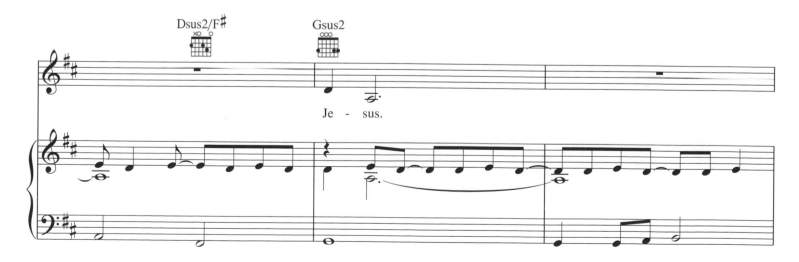

Je - sus.

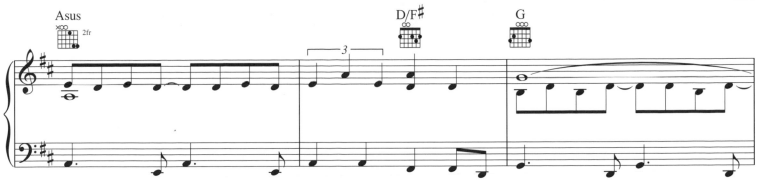

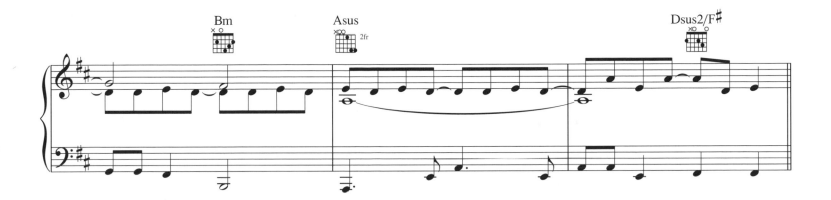

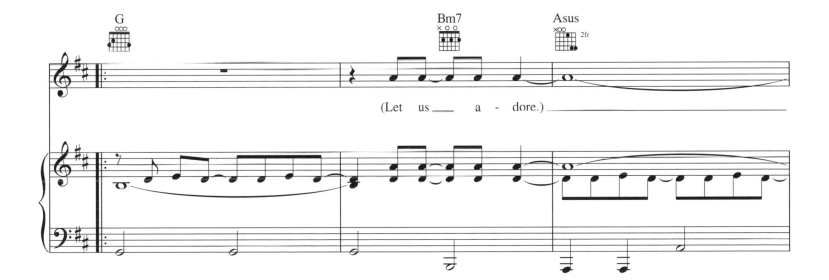

(Let us ___ a - dore.) _____

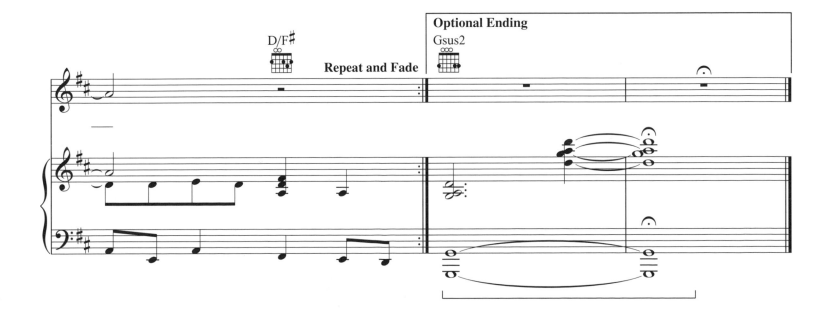

O COME, O COME EMMANUEL

Words Translated by JOHN M. NEALE and HENRY S. COFFIN
Music by STEVEN CURTIS CHAPMAN

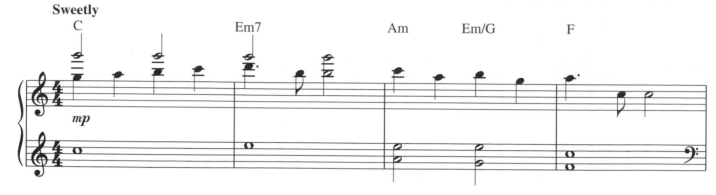

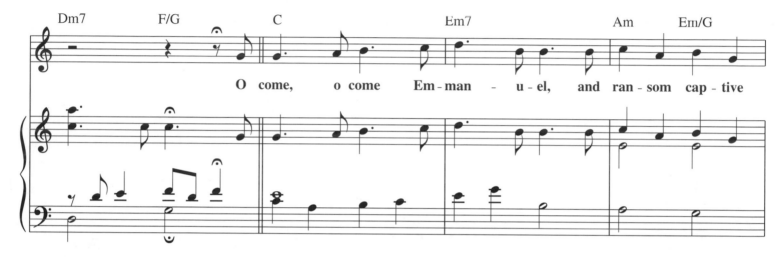

O come, o come Em-man - u - el, and ran - som cap - tive

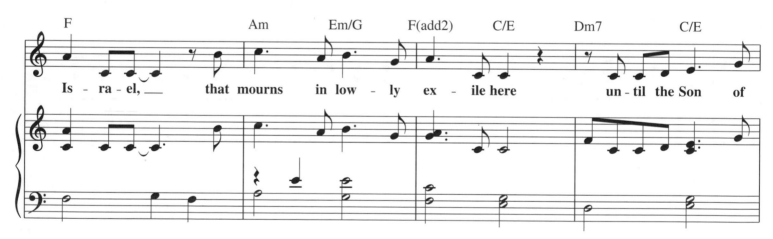

Is - ra - el, ___ that mourns in low - ly ex - ile here un - til the Son of

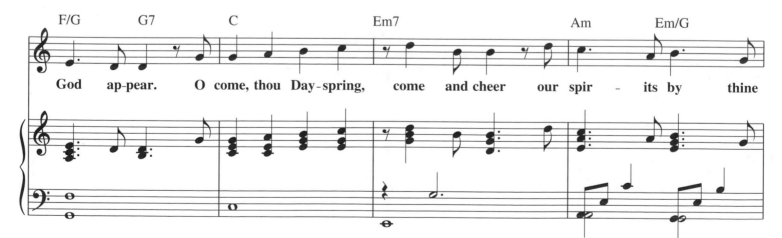

God ap-pear. O come, thou Day-spring, come and cheer our spir - its by thine

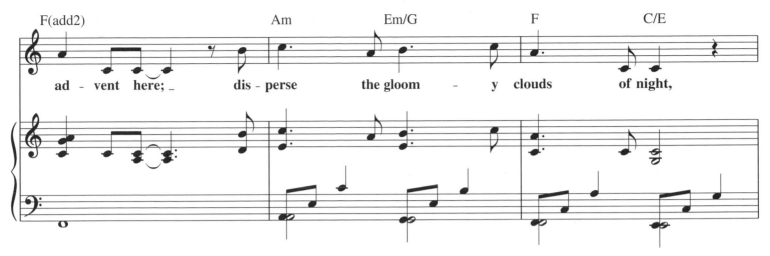

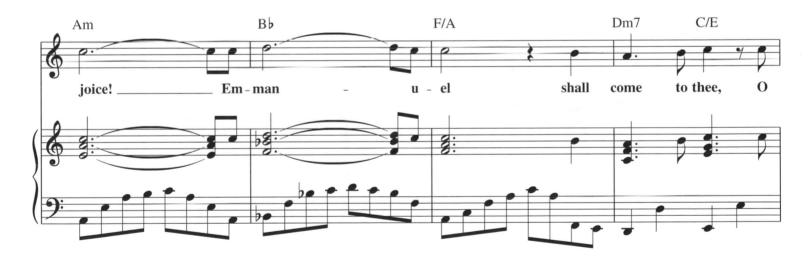

el shall come to thee, O Is-ra-el! Re-joice! _____

Oh, re-

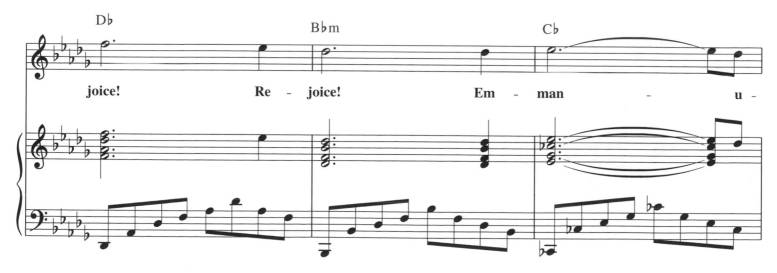

joice! Re-joice! Em-man-u-

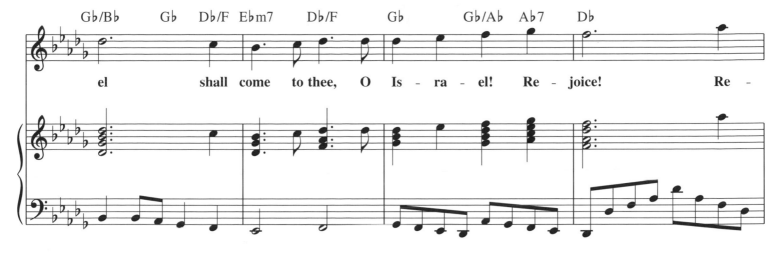

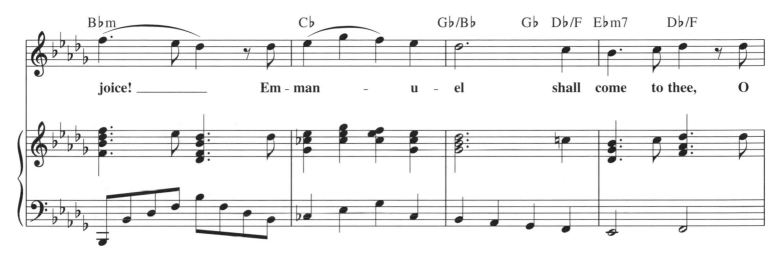

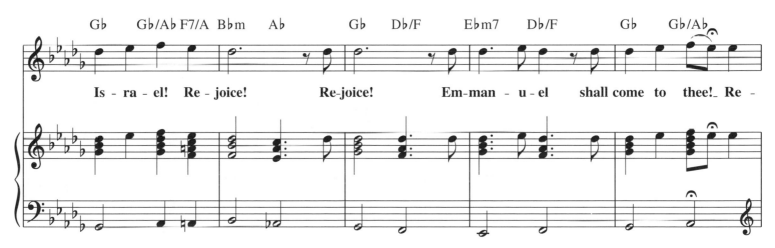

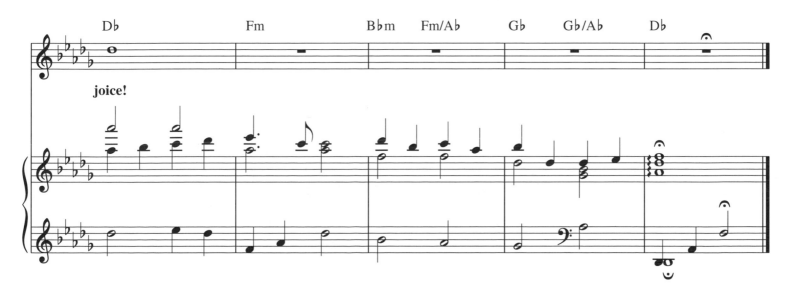

ONE SMALL CHILD

Words and Music by
DAVID MEECE

OUR BLESSED SAVIOR CAME

Words and Music by
CARMAN

Expressively

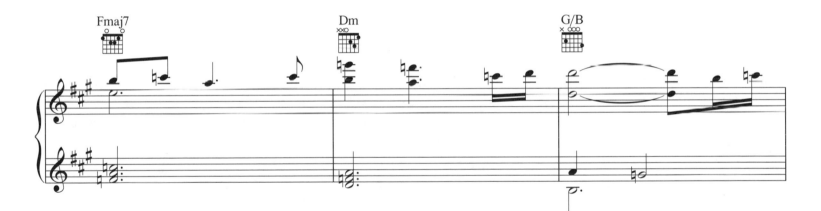

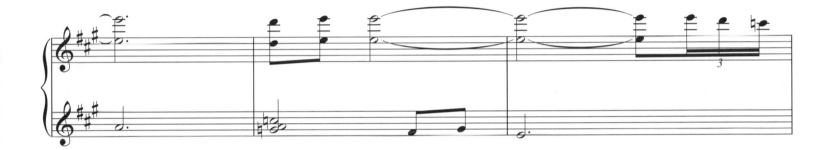

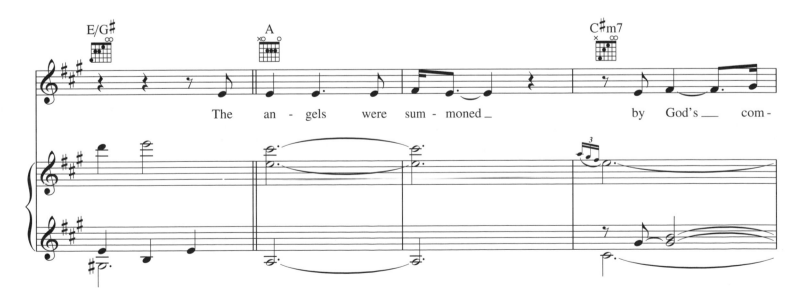

The an-gels were sum-moned _____ by God's _____ com-

mand, _____ the ver - dict de - liv - ered _ for sal - va - tion's plan. _

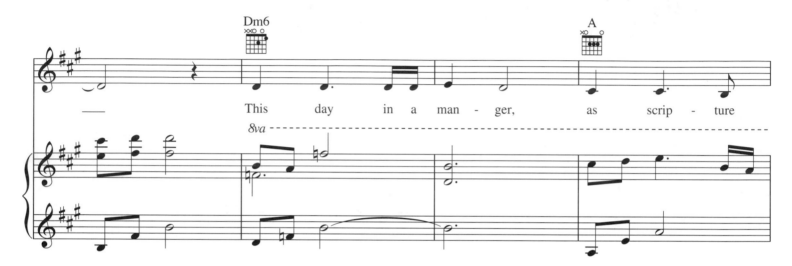

_ This day in a man - ger, as scrip - ture

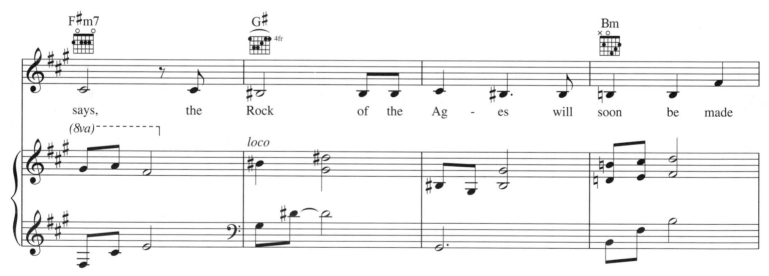

says, the Rock of the Ag - es will soon be made

flesh. _ The time that was cho - sen _ by God's per - fect
love nev - er great - er, _ to this world He gave. _

glo - ry to God in the high -

est!" Sing - ing, ___ sing - ing they came, ___

prais - ing and mag - ni - fy - ing His

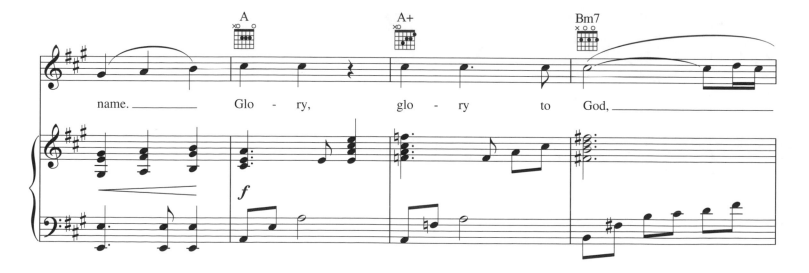

name. ___ Glo - ry, glo - ry to God, ___

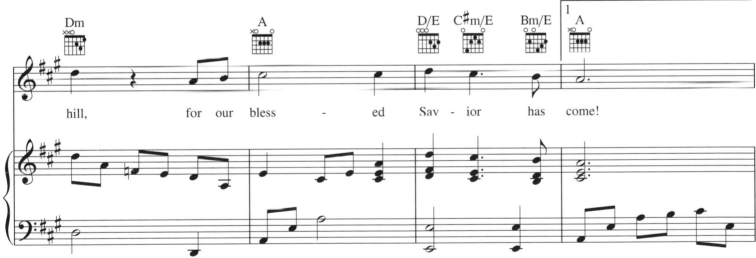

come!   The skies _____ were a-

live   with their glo - ry; _____   the shep-herds stood

gaz - ing __ in fear. _____   The song of the

an - gels   rang   out   with   au - thor - i - ty: ___   The

Sing - ing, ___ sing - ing ___ they came, _____

prais - ing and mag - ni - fy - ing His name. _____

Glo - ry, glo - ry to God, _____

glo - ry to God in the high - est!

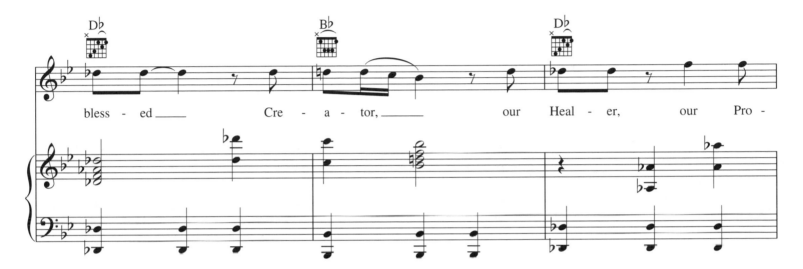

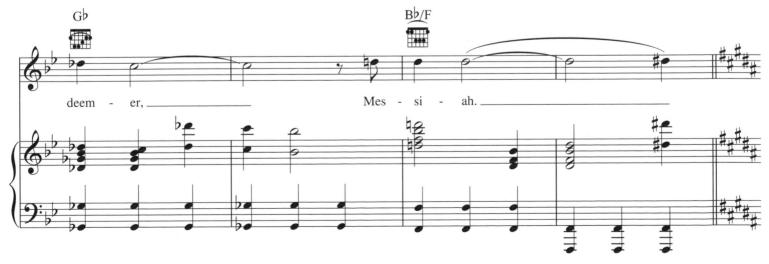

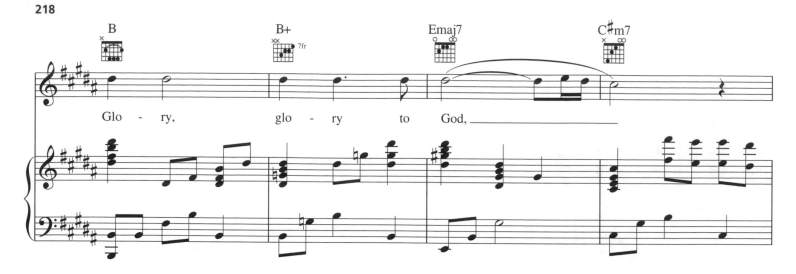

Glory, glory to God,

glory to God in the high - est!

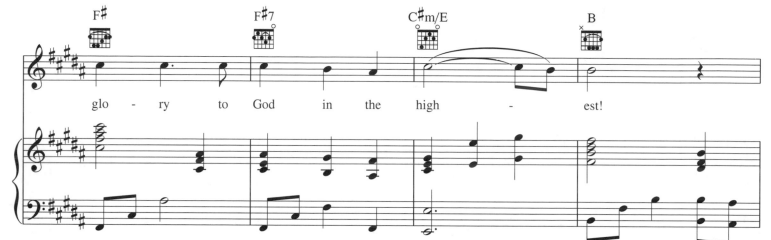

"Peace and good will" the shep - herds heard from the hill,

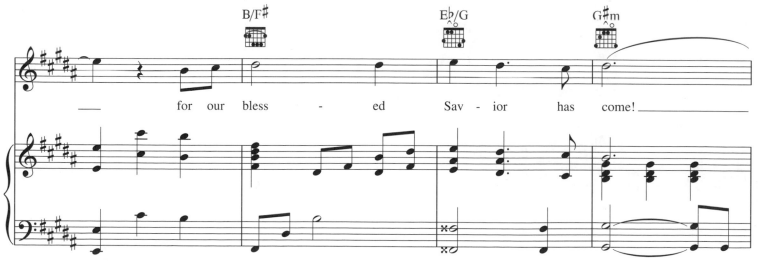

for our bless - ed Sav - ior has come!

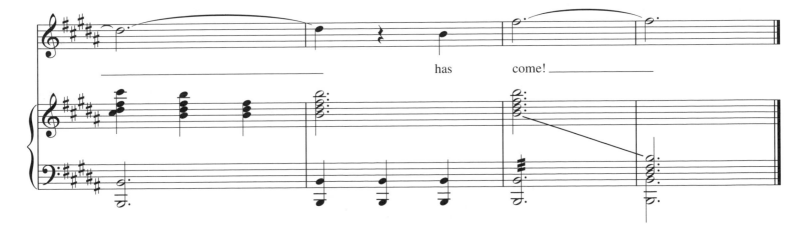

OUR GOD IS WITH US

Words and Music by STEVEN CURTIS CHAPMAN
and MICHAEL W. SMITH

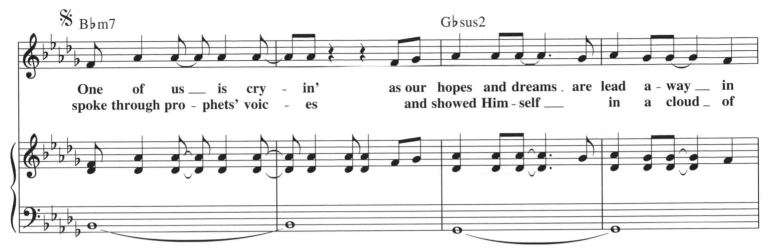

One of us __ is cry - in' as our hopes and dreams __ are lead a - way __ in
spoke through pro - phets' voic - es and showed Him - self __ in a cloud __ of

chains and we're left __ all __ a - lone. And
fire. No one had seen His face un -

one of us __ is dy - in' as our love is slow - ly low - ered in __ the grave, __
til the one __ most ho - ly re - vealed to us __ His per - fect heart's de - sire __

oh, __ and we're left on __ our own. __ But for
and left His right - ful place. __ And

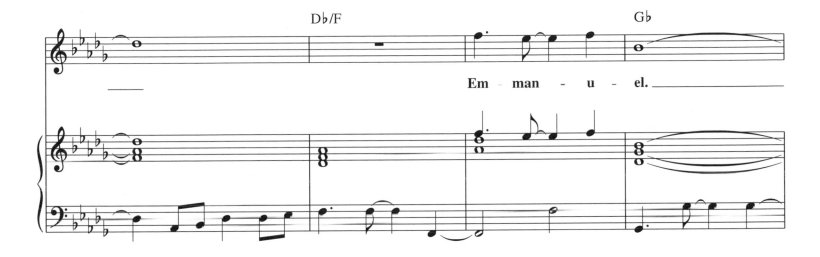

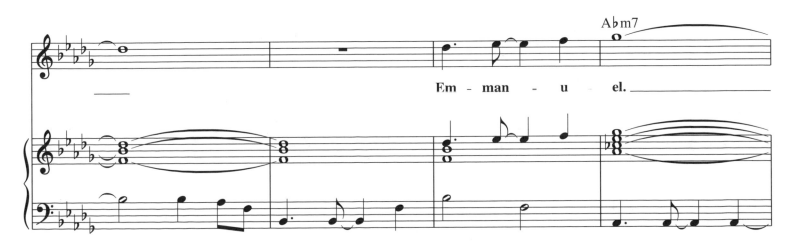

And we will nev-er

face life a - lone now that God has

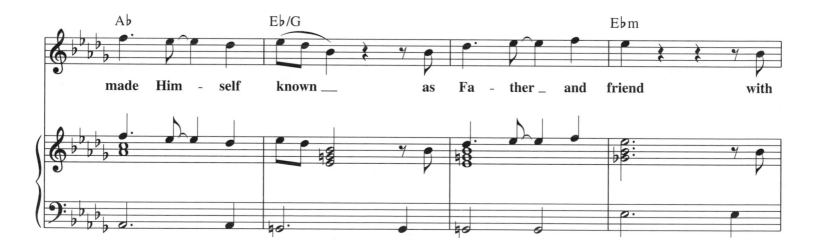

made Him - self known as Fa - ther and friend with

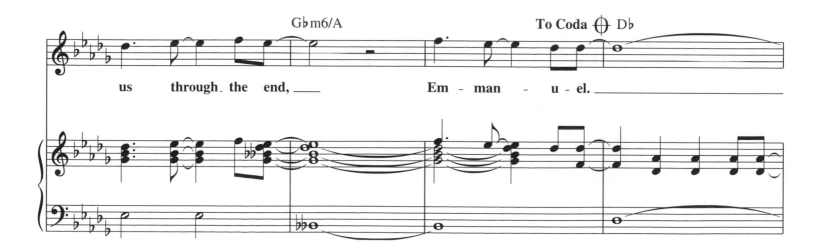

us through the end, Em - man - u - el.

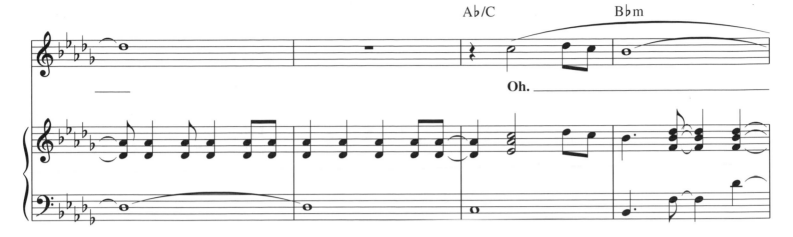

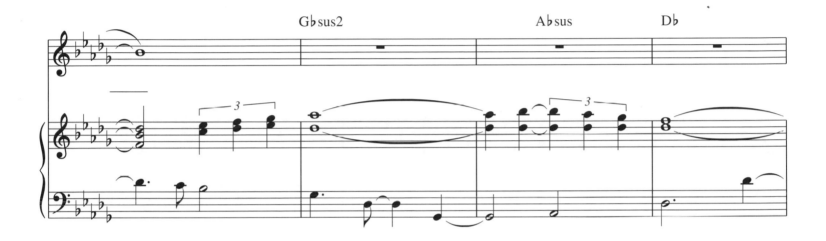

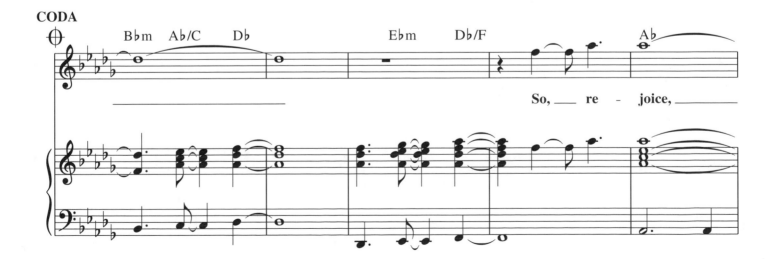

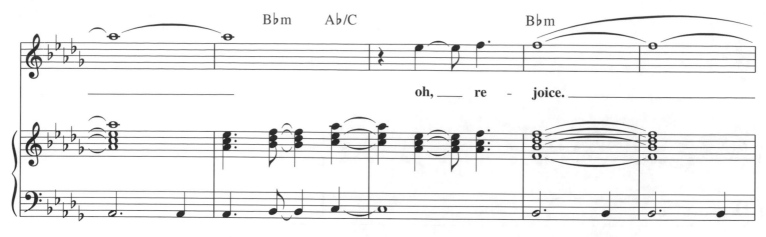

oh, ___ re - joice.

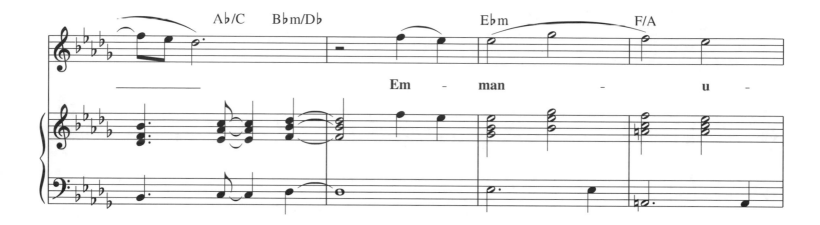

Em - man - u -

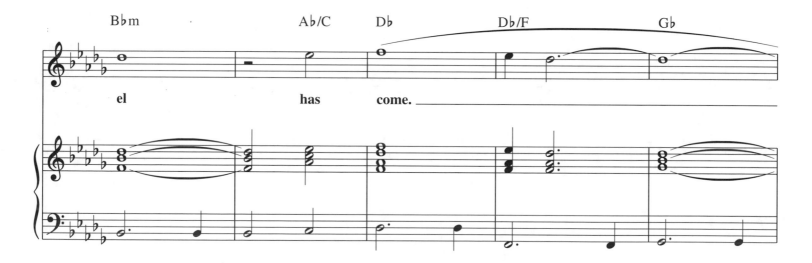

el ___ has come. ___

And our God _ is with us, _

D/F#   G

Em - man - u - el.

Em6/B   Bm

He's come to save us,

Am7

Em - man - u - el.

D7/F#   G

And we will nev - er

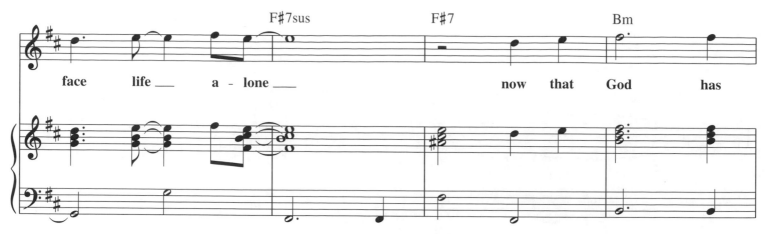

face life __ a - lone __ now that God has

made him - self known ____ as Fa - ther _ and friend, with

us to the end, Em - man - u - el. _____

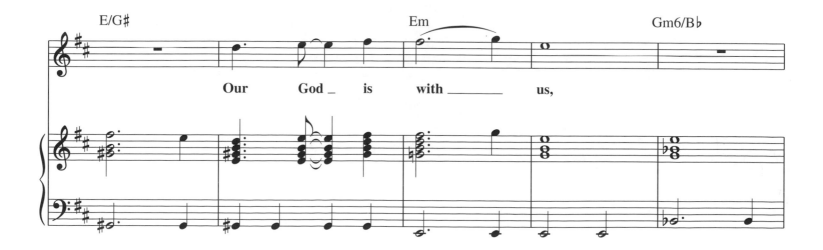

Our God _ is with _____ us,

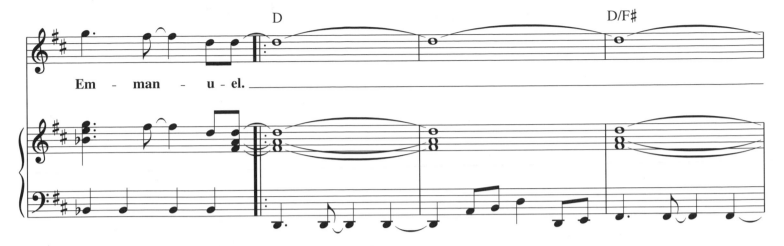

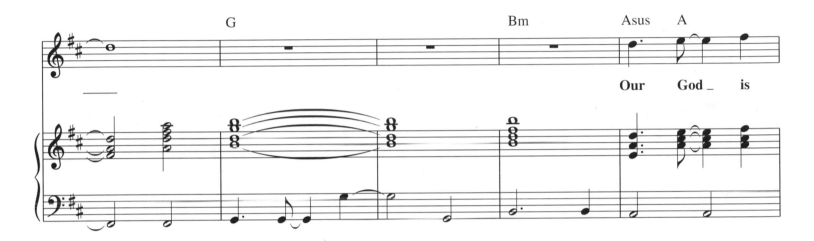

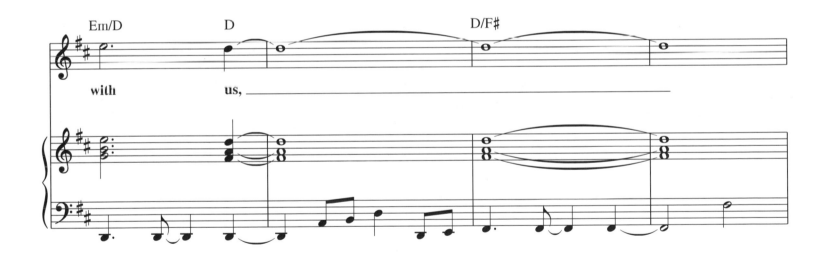

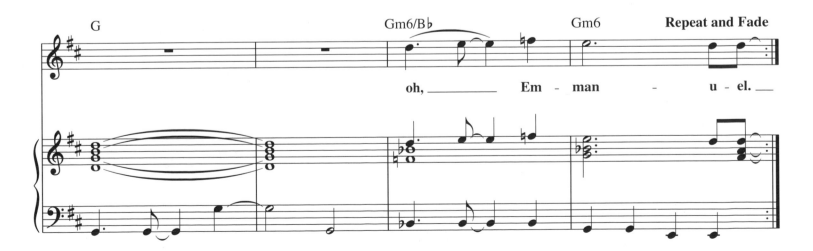

PRECIOUS PROMISE

Words and Music by
STEVEN CURTIS CHAPMAN

Quietly

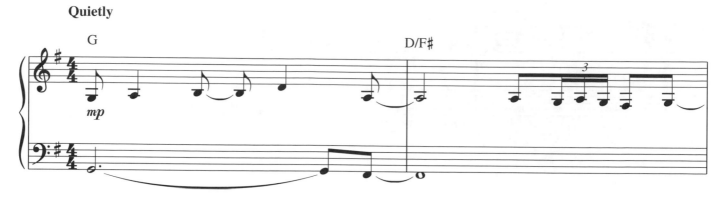

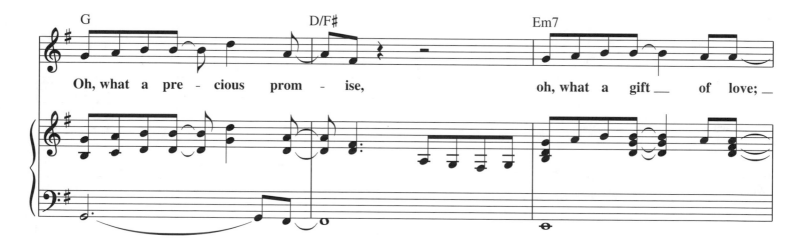

Oh, what a pre - cious prom - ise, oh, what a gift __ of love; __

__ an an - gel tells __ a vir - gin that __

are met with an
when she's al-read-y car-
to roll back the cur-

o-ver-whelm-ing joy ___ that God has chos-en ___ her.
-ry-ing ___ a child ___ that is-n't ___ his ___ own. ___
-tain ___ and un-veil ___ His pas-sion for ___ the heart of

man.

Oh, what a pre-cious prom-

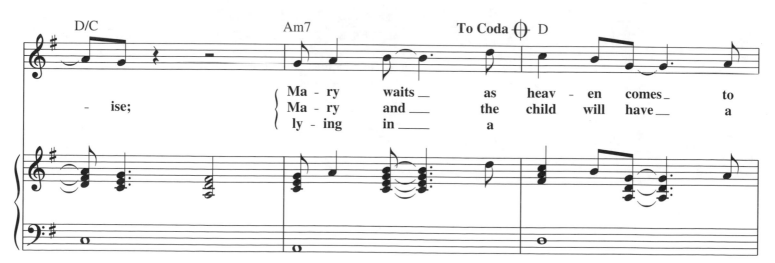

-ise;
Ma-ry waits ___ as heav-en comes ___ to
Ma-ry and ___ the child will have ___ a
ly-ing in ___ a

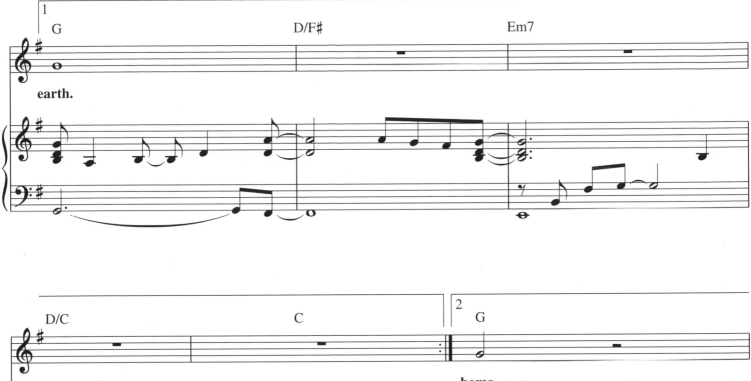

earth.

home.

And shep - herds _ stand on ___ a

hill - side, ___ their _ hearts rac - ing with _ the news _

the an - gel told them.

A

star's light ___ fills up ___ the dark sky ___

as the night of pre - cious prom - ise is un -

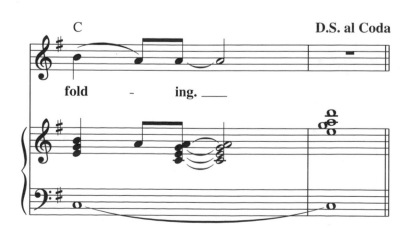

fold - ing. ___

D.S. al Coda

CODA

man - ger in Beth - le - hem.

Oh, what a pre - cious prom -

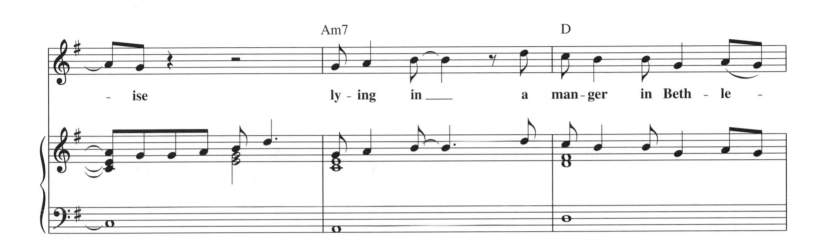

- ise ly - ing in _____ a man - ger in Beth - le -

hem.

ROSE OF BETHLEHEM

Words and Music by
LOWELL ALEXANDER

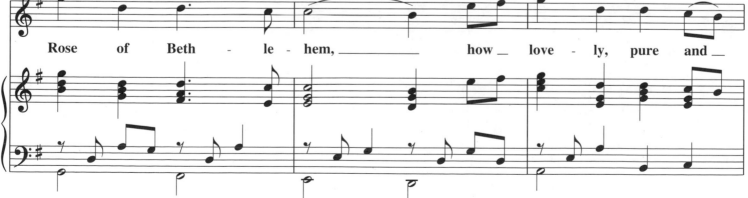

STILL HER LITTLE CHILD

Words and Music by RAY BOLTZ
and STEVE MILLIKAN

With intensity ♩ = 74

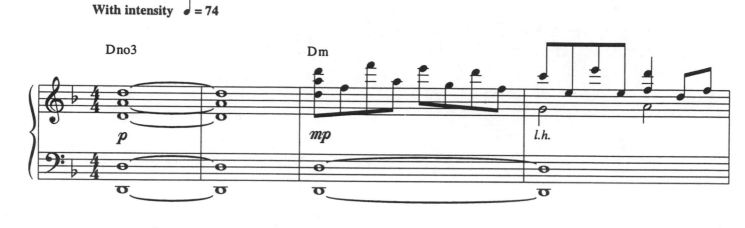

When she laid Him in the

man - ger, He was still her lit - tle child. In a

cit - y filled with strang - ers, He was still her lit - tle

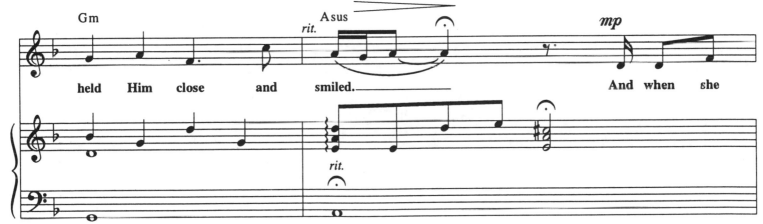

child. Though the inn was full and the night was cold, she

held Him close and smiled._____ And when she

laid Him in the man - ger, He was still her lit - tle

child.   2. When the an - gel called Him

Sav - ior,   He was   still   her   lit - tle   child.   When the

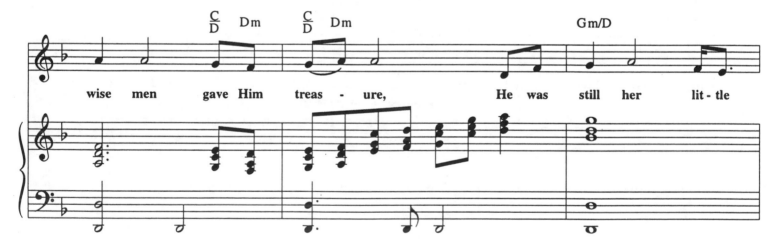

wise   men   gave Him   treas - ure,   He was   still   her   lit - tle

child.   When the   shep - herds bowed be - fore— Him,   a

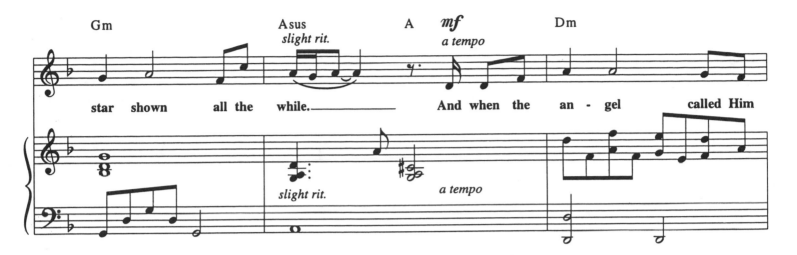

star shown all the while._____ And when the an - gel called Him

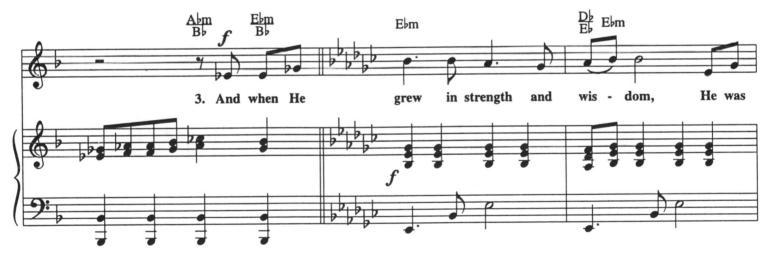

Sav - ior, He was still her lit - tle child.

3. And when He grew in strength and wis - dom, He was

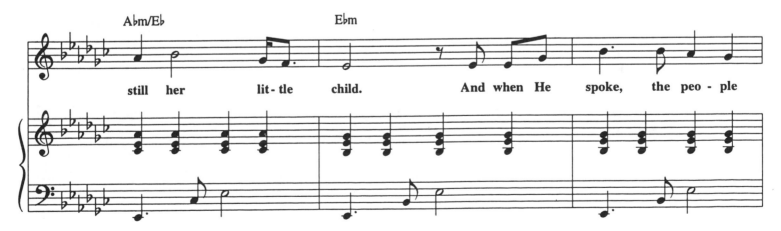

still her lit - tle child. And when He spoke, the peo - ple

lis - tened; but He was still her lit- tle child. And when He

healed the lame and dy - ing, they would fol - low Him for

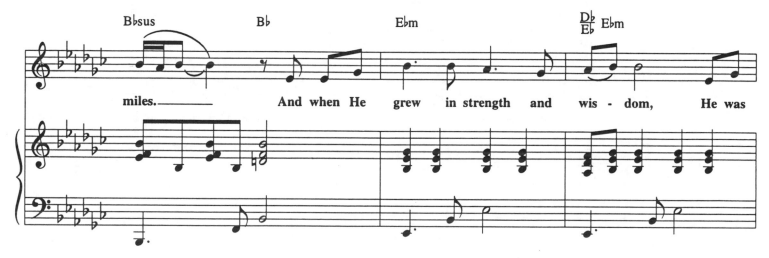

miles._____ And when He grew in strength and wis - dom, He was

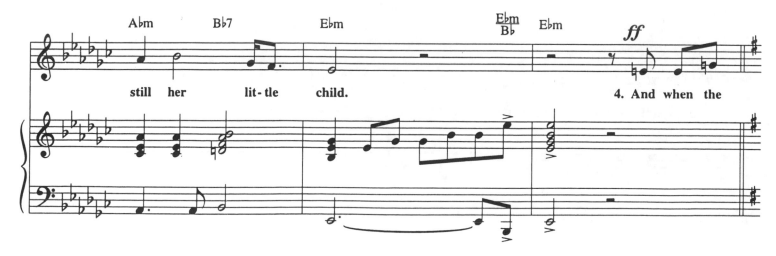

still her lit- tle child. 4. And when the

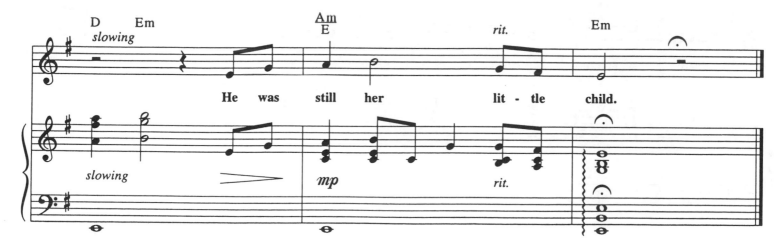

A STRANGE WAY TO SAVE THE WORLD

Words and Music by DAVE CLARK,
MARK HARRIS and DON KOCH

'Cause nev - er in a mil - lion lives_____
There would have been no Beth - le - hem,_____

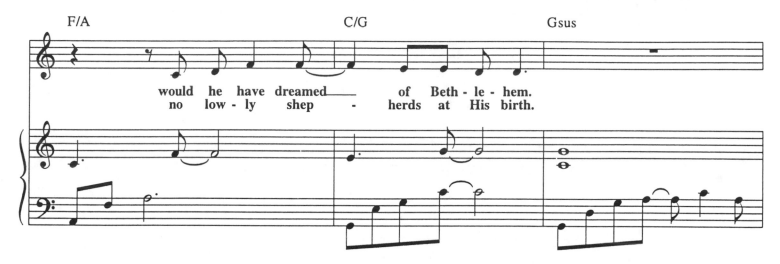

would he have dreamed_____ of Beth - le - hem.
no low - ly shep - herds at His birth.

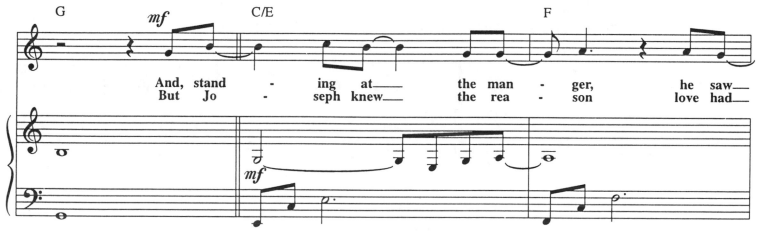

And, stand - ing at_____ the man - ger, he saw_____
But Jo - seph knew_____ the rea - son love had_____

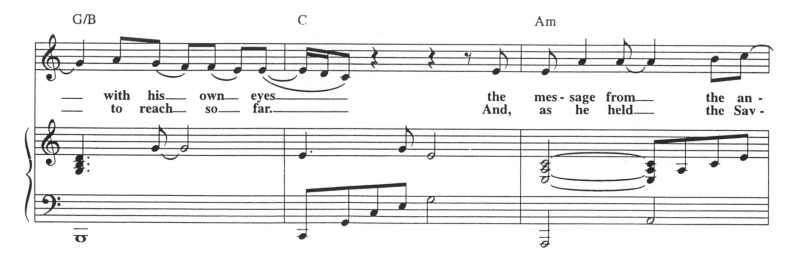

_____ with his_____ own_ eyes_____ the mes - sage from_____ the an -
_____ to reach_ so_ far._____ And, as he held_____ the Sav -

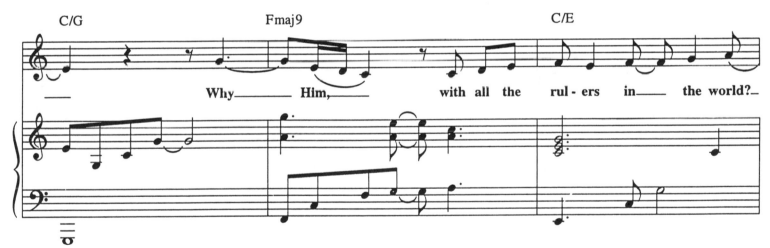

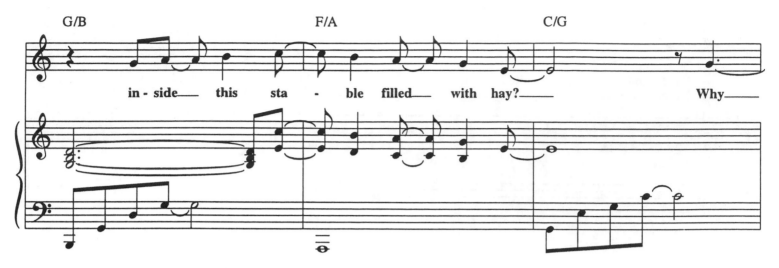

in - side this sta - ble filled with hay? Why

her? She's just an or - di - nar - y girl."

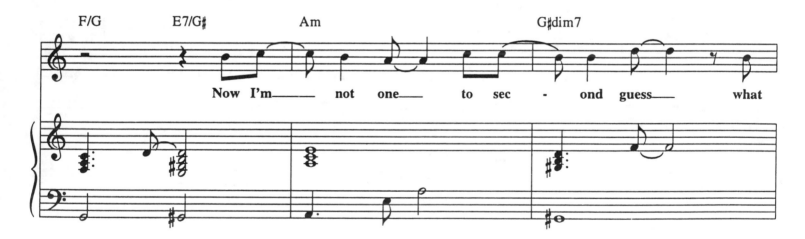

Now I'm not one to sec - ond guess what

an - gels have to say, but this is such a

strange___ way_____ to save___ the world._____

2. To think of how it

Oh____

Now I'm___ not one___ to sec -

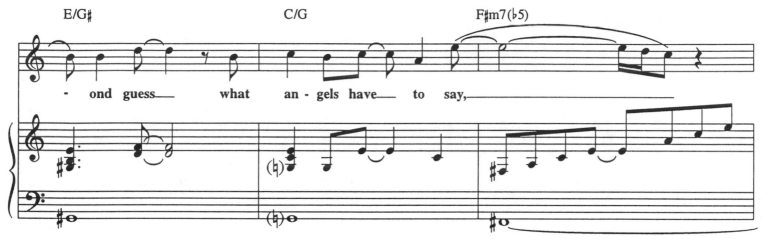

- ond guess___ what an - gels have to say,___

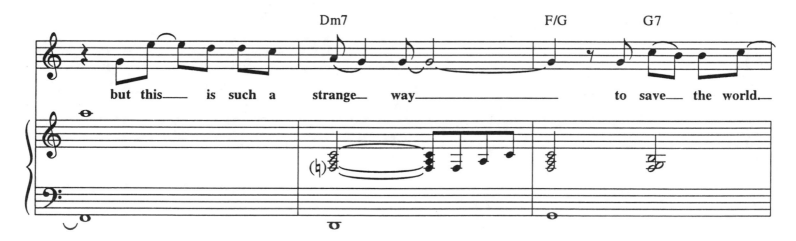

but this___ is such a strange___ way___ to save___ the world.___

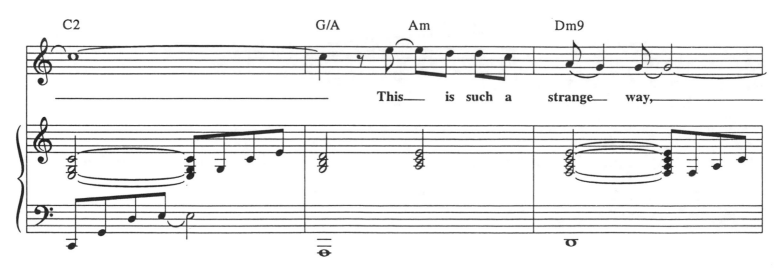

This___ is such a strange___ way,___

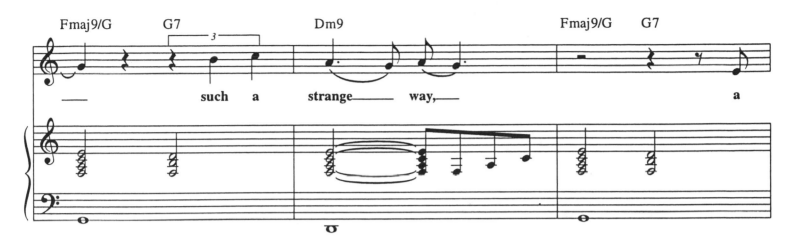

such a strange_____ way,_____ a

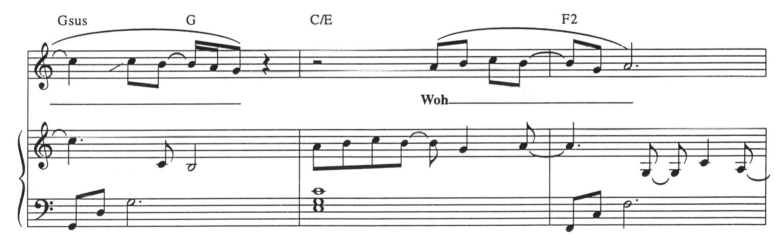

strange_____ way to save_____ the world._____

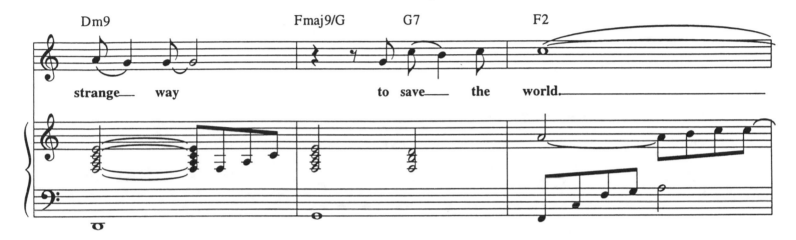

_____ Woh_____

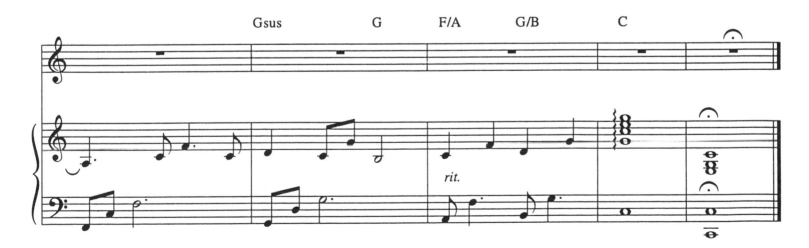

THIS BABY

Words and Music by
STEVEN CURTIS CHAPMAN

Gently

What child is this, __ who, laid to rest, __ on Ma - ry's lap __ is sleep - ing? Whom an - gels greet __ with an - thems sweet, __ while shep - herds watch __ are keep - ing?

Rhythmically

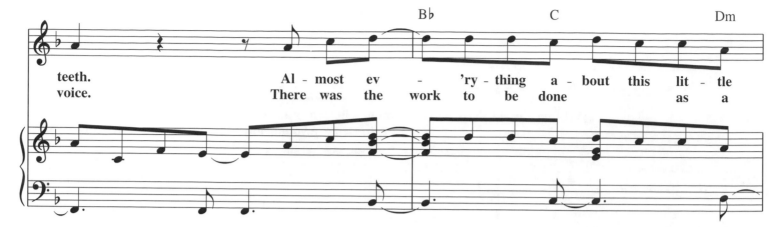

teeth.
voice.

Al - most ev - 'ry - thing a - bout this lit - tle
There was the work to be done as a

ba - by seemed as nat - u - ral as it could __ be.
car - pen - ter's son, and all the neigh - bors said he's such a fine boy.

But this {(1., D.S.) ba - by / boy __} made the an - gels sing, _____ and this {ba - by / boy __} made a

new star shine __ in the sky. ___ This {ba - by / boy __} had come __ to change __ the world. __

This {ba - by / boy __} was God's __ own Son. ____

This {ba - by / boy __} was like __ no __ oth - er one. This {ba - by / boy __} was God __

____ with us. ____ This ba - by was Je - sus. ____

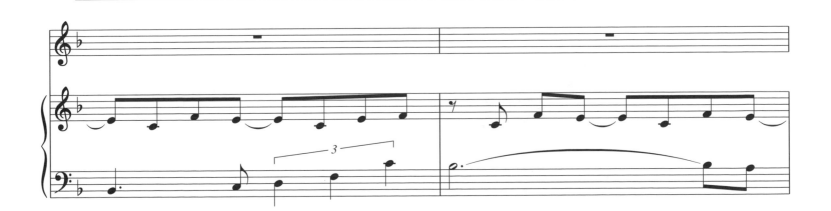

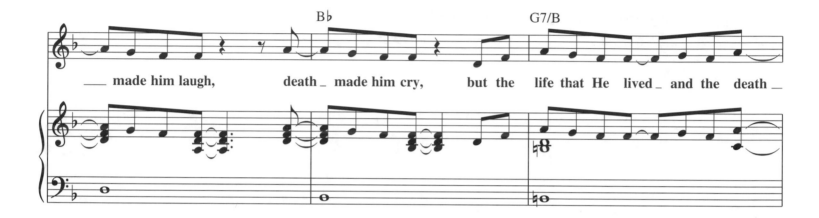

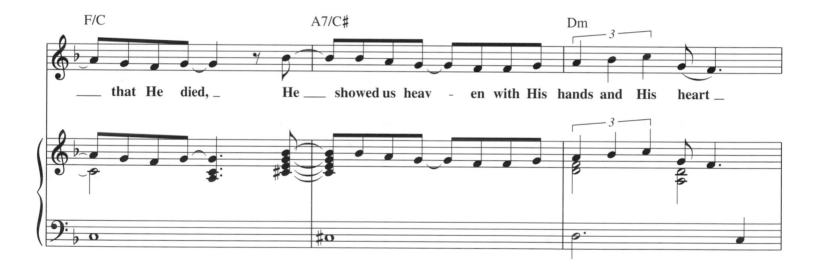

no oth - er one; ho - ly and pure right from the

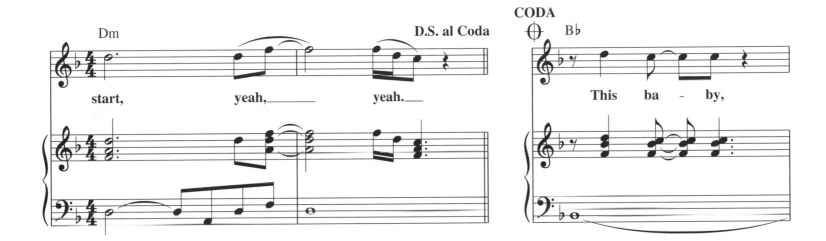

start, yeah,_____ yeah.____ **CODA** This ba - by,

this ba - by was Je - sus._____

Repeat and Fade

This ba - by was Je -

THIS GIFT

Words and Music by STEVE AMERSON
and DAVID T. CLYDESDALE

Light pop feel ♩ = 104

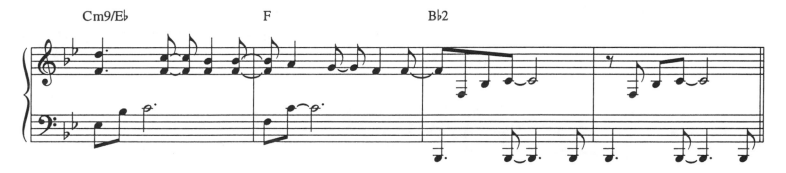

This gift— was the great-est gift— that the world had ev - er known.—

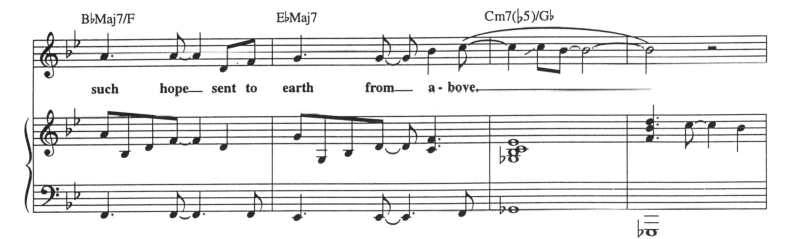

wrapped in heav - en's love.___ What can I give to some -

- one who's hurt - ing? What can you share___ to calm a

trou - bled heart?___ In this sea - son of hope just___ what___ can you of - fer to

some - one whose life is torn a - part?___ Oh, the dreams of all___ e -

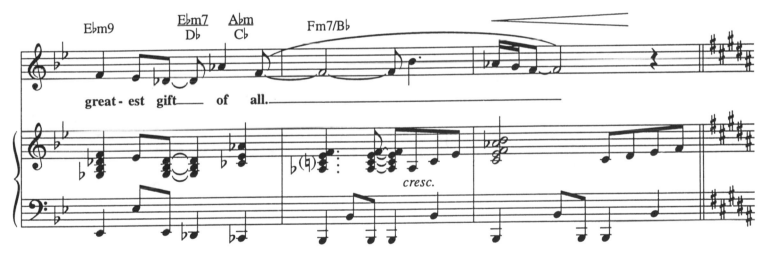

God's love—— in the form of—— a lit - tle

Child—— from—— heav - en's throne.——————— Such joy,——

such hope—— sent to earth from—— a - bove.——

This gift,—— God's great - est gift.——

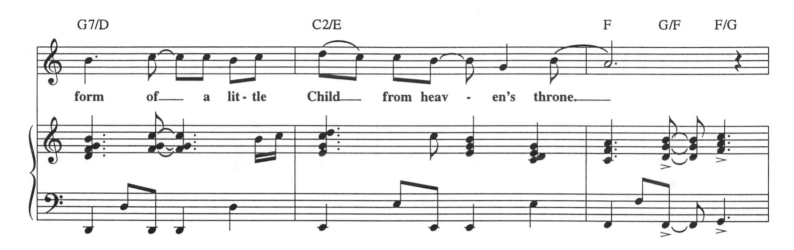

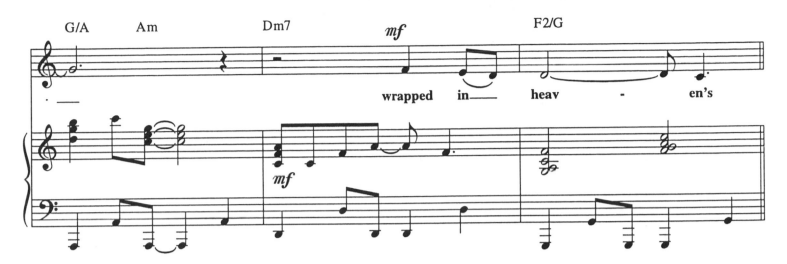

THIS LITTLE CHILD

Words and Music by
SCOTT WESLEY BROWN

Moderately slow, in 2

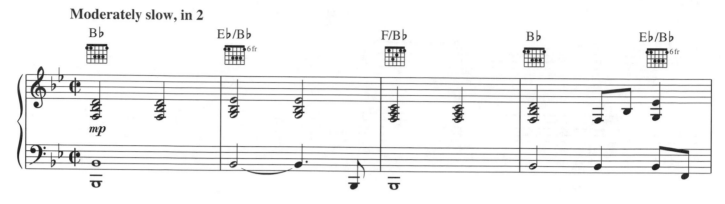

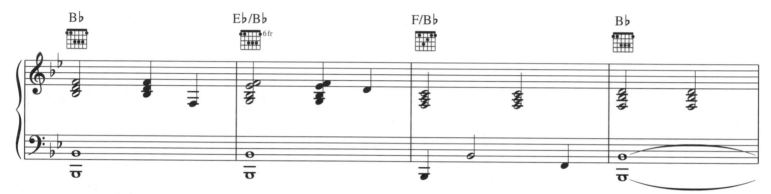

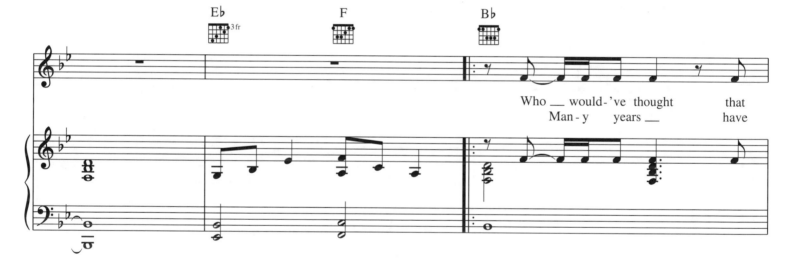

Who __ would-'ve thought   that
Man-y years __ have

long a-go,   so ver-y far __ a-way,
come and gone,   yet this world re - mains __ the same.

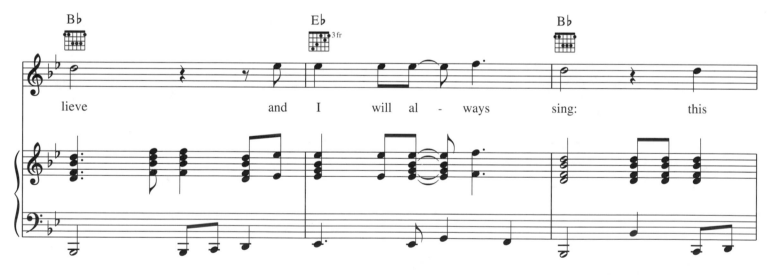

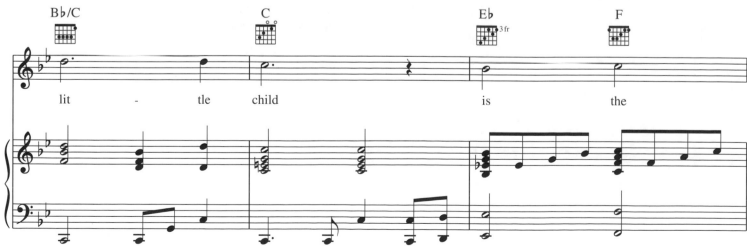

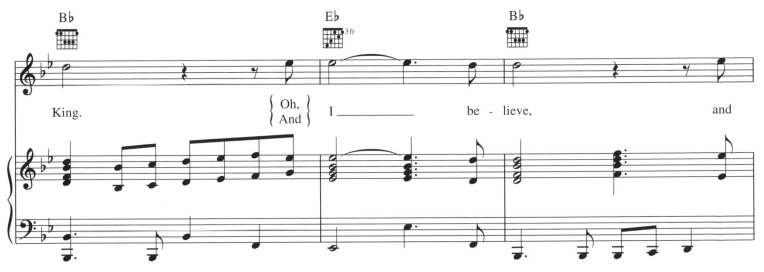

King. Oh, / And I _____ be - lieve, and

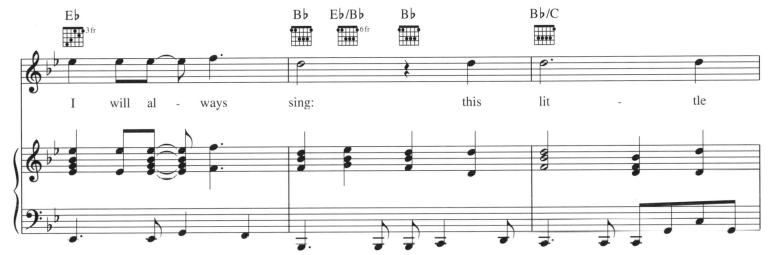

I will al - ways sing: this lit - tle

child, He is the ___ King of

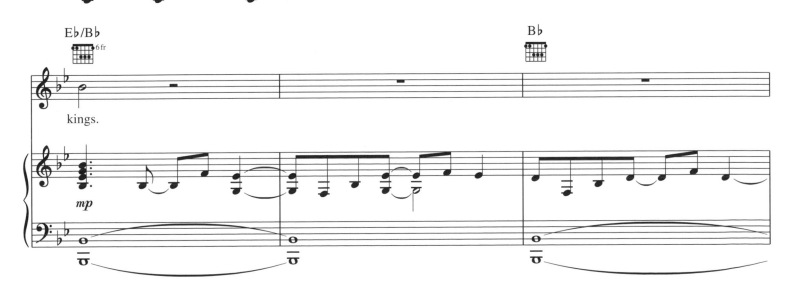

kings.

mp

long a - go, ___ so ver - y far ___ a - way, ___ this

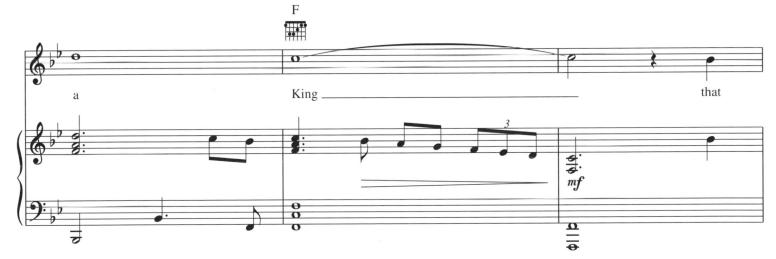

lit - tle child, ___ our on - ly hope, ___ was born

a   King _____   that

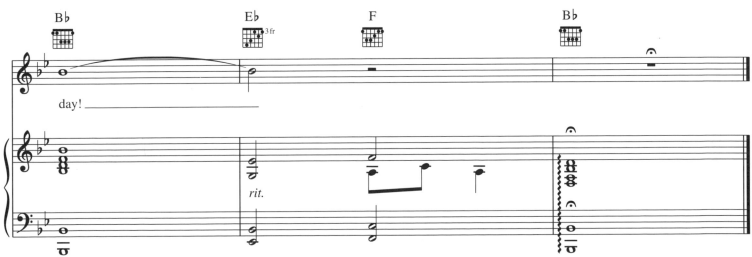

day! _____

TO THE MYSTERY

Words and Music by
MICHAEL CARD

In two, with a beat ♩ = 80

1. When the Fa - ther longed to show a love He want -
2. No fic - tion as fan - tas - tic and wild, a moth - er made
3. Be - cause the fall did dev - as - tate, Cre - a - tor must

Opt. harmony: 2nd and 3rd times only

*Note: Optional harmony should be sung at actual pitches, whether male or female solo.

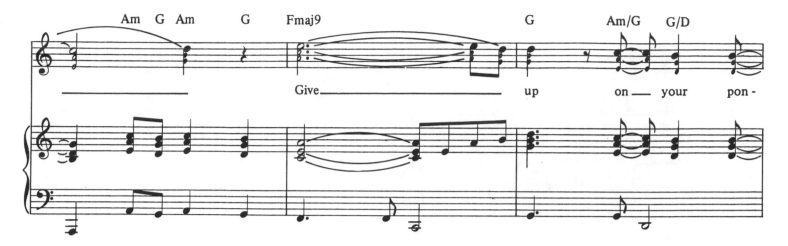

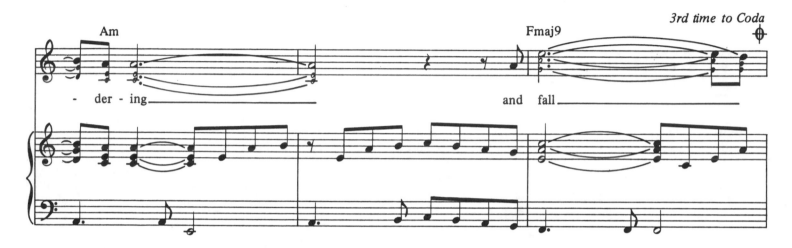

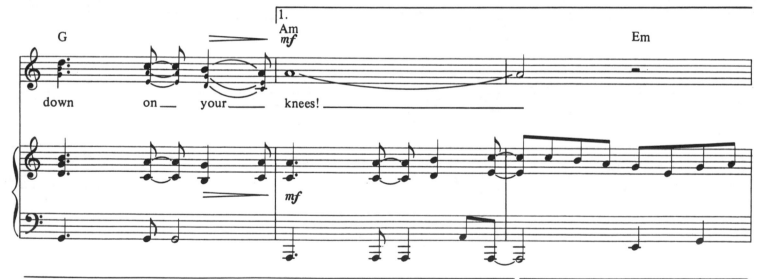

Acoustic guitar solo

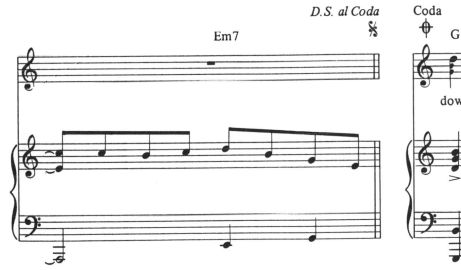

D.S. al Coda

Coda

down   on   your

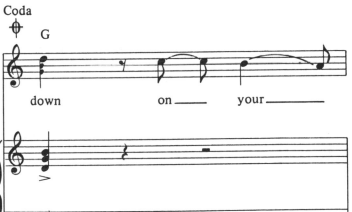

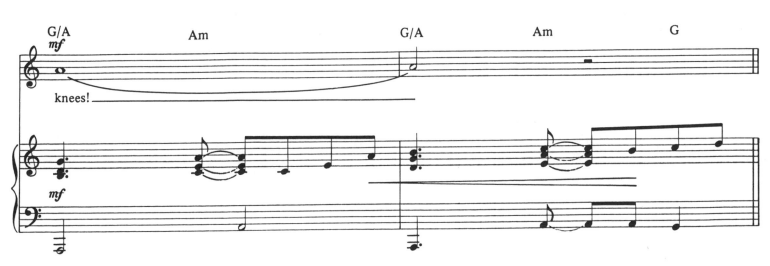

knees!

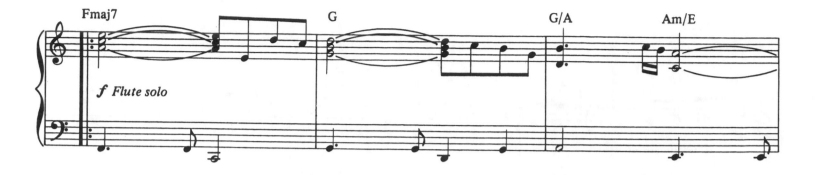

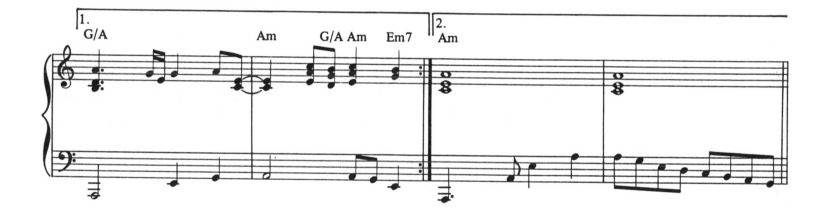

Oh, _____ that is __ the mys - ter - y, _____

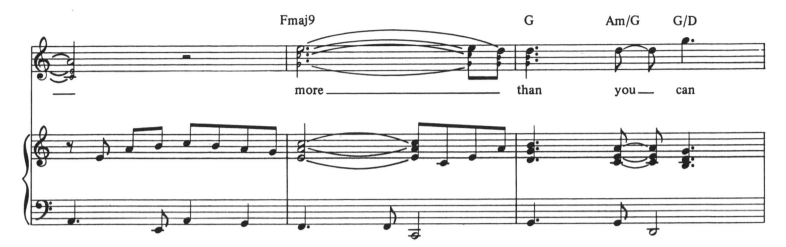

more _____ than you _ can

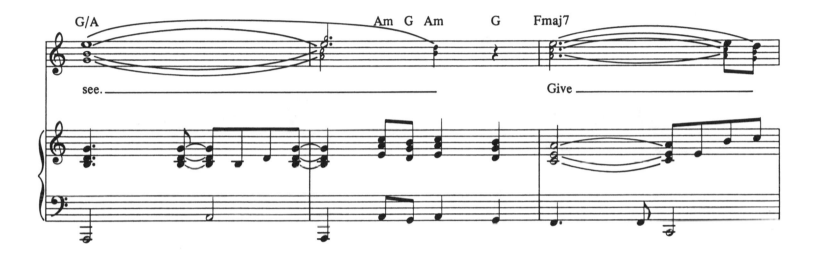

see. _____ Give _____

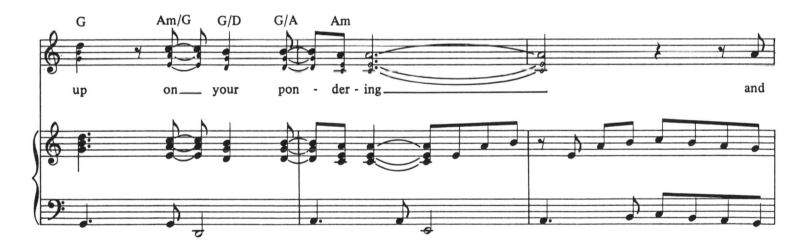

up on _ your pon - der - ing _____ and

Repeat and fade

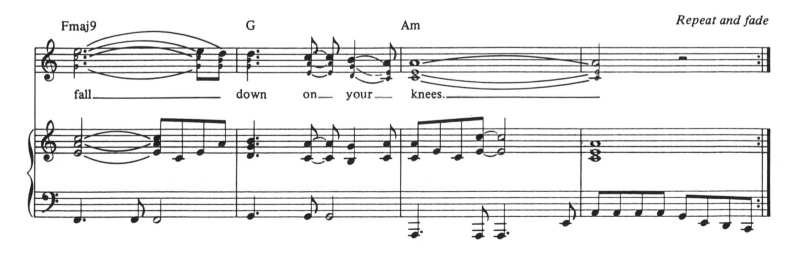

fall _____ down on your _ knees. _____

UNTO US
(Isaiah 9)

Words and Music by LARRY BRYANT
and LESA BRYANT

Peo - ple____ who walk in the dark - ness____ are
boot that____ has marched to the bat - tle____ will

going to___ be-hold a great____ light;_____
fin - al - ly be set a - flame;_____

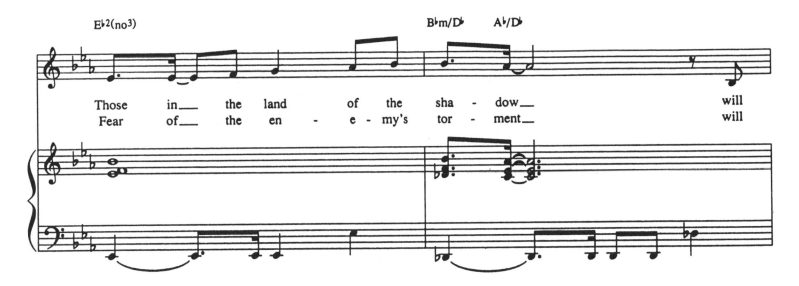

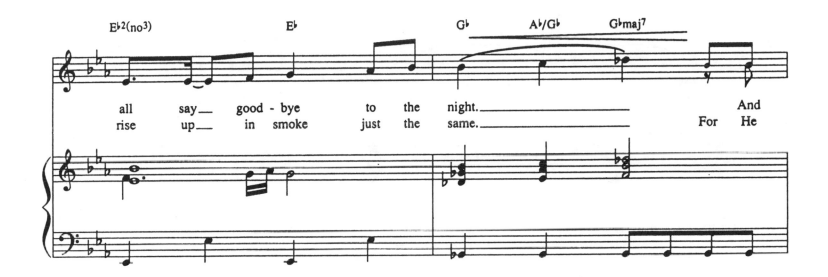

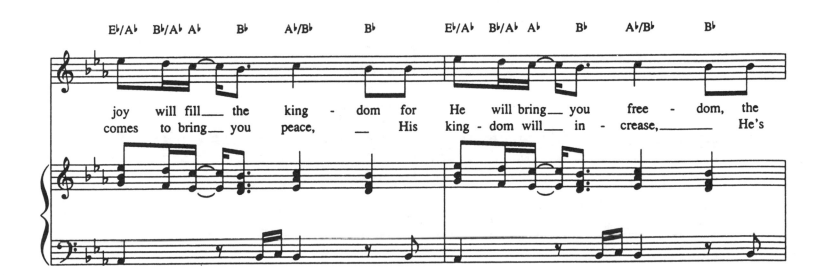

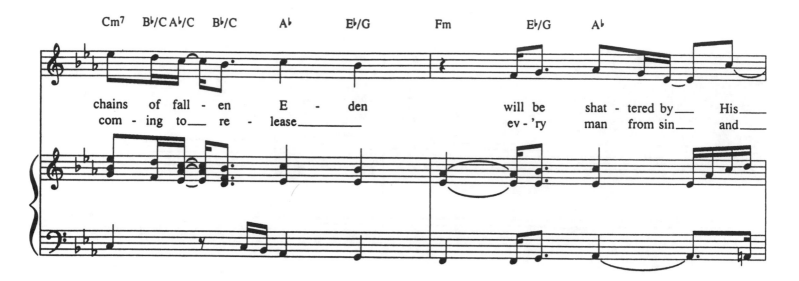

chains of fall - en E - den will be shat - tered by___ His___
com - ing to___ re - lease_____ ev - 'ry man from sin___ and___

___ might.___
___ shame.___

Un - to us___ a child___ is born

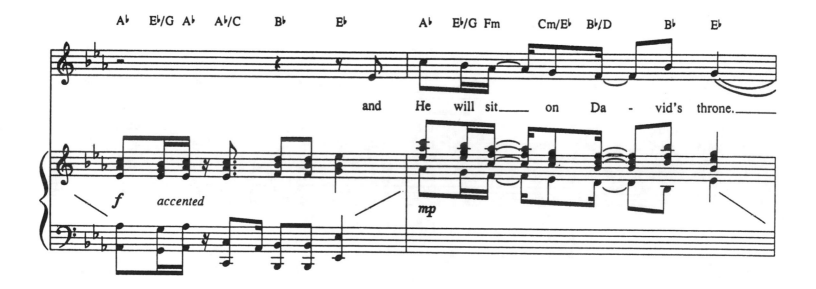

and He will sit___ on Da - vid's throne.___

WE ARE THE REASON

Words and Music by
DAVID MEECE

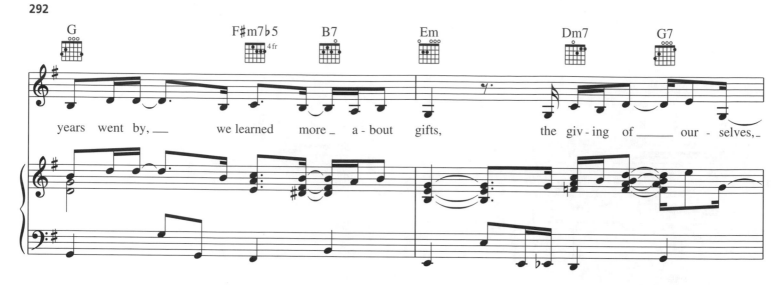

years went by, __ we learned more _ a-bout gifts, the giv-ing of ____ our - selves, __

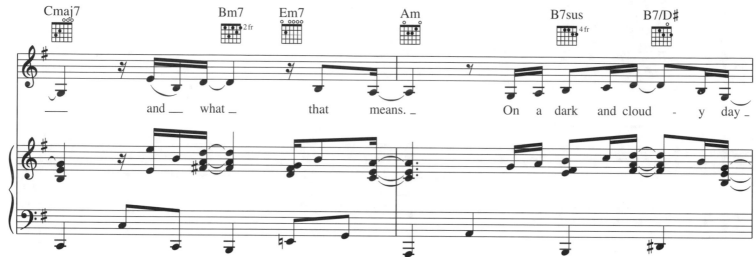

__ and __ what __ that means. _ On a dark and cloud - y day __

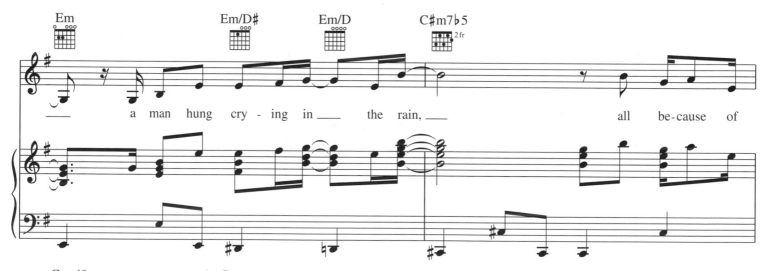

__ a man hung cry - ing in ___ the rain, ___ all be-cause of

love, all be-cause of love. _____ Oh, __ and

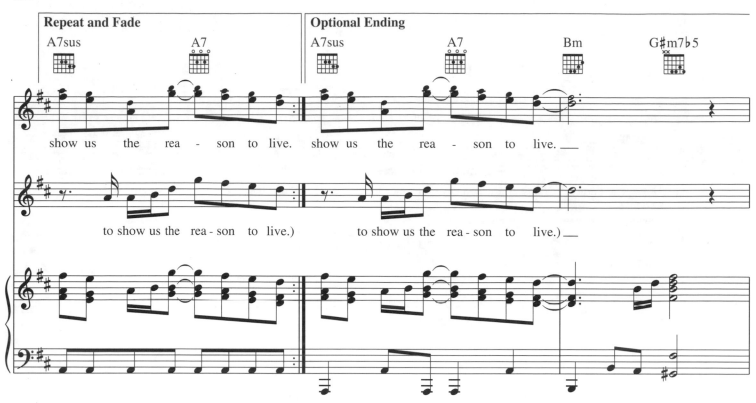

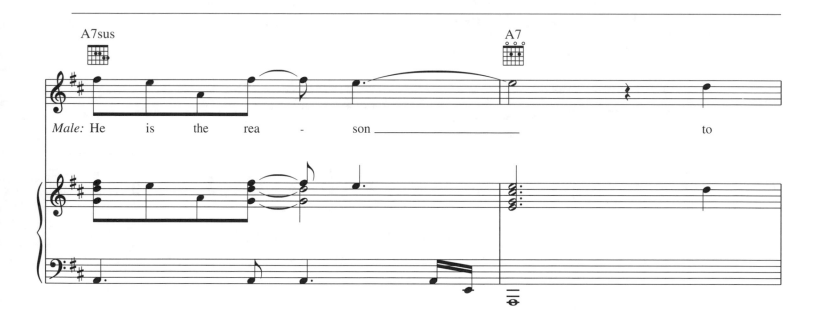

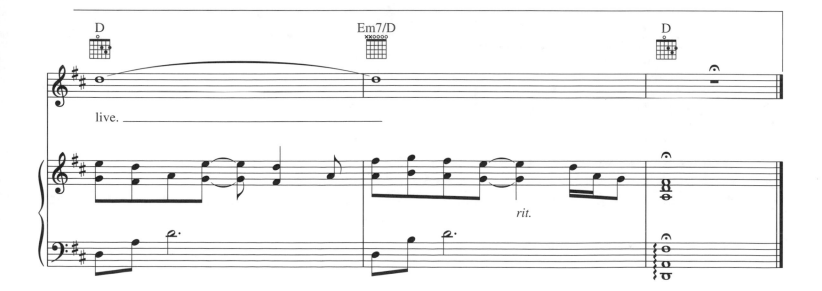

WHEN HER EYES ARE ON THE CHILD

Words and Music by RAY BOLTZ
and STEVE MILLIKAN

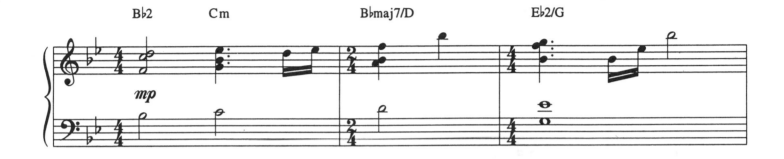

1. There's a

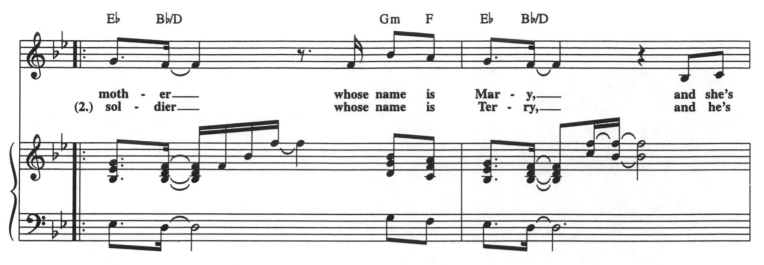

moth - er___ whose name is Mar - y,___ and she's
(2.) sol - dier___ whose name is Ter - ry,___ and he's

trav - eled ver - y far.___ But she's not
serv - ing far from home.___ It's the

think - ing___ a - bout her jour - ney___ now, there's a
first time___ that he's spent Christ - mas___ far a -

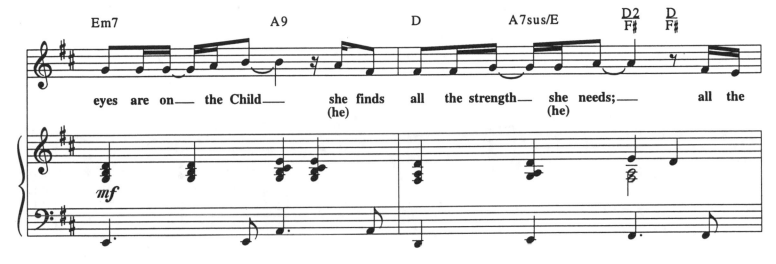

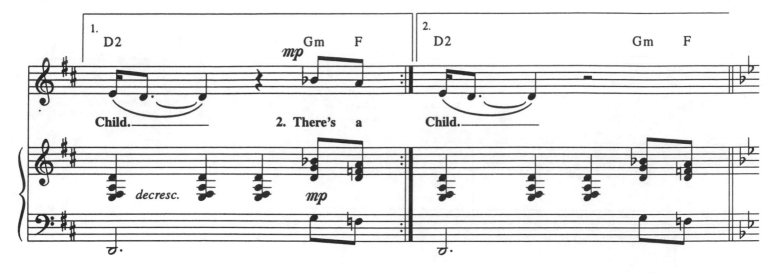

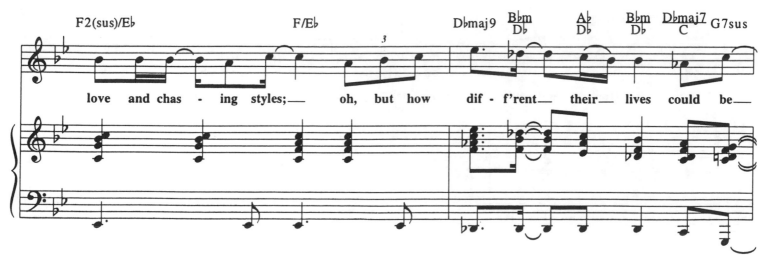

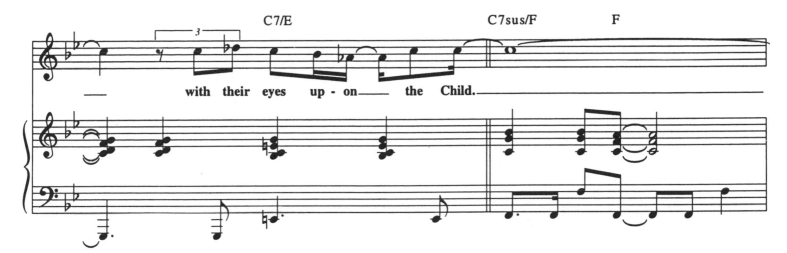

with their eyes up - on_____ the Child._____

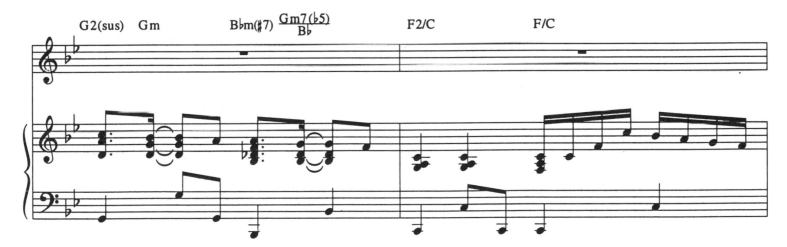

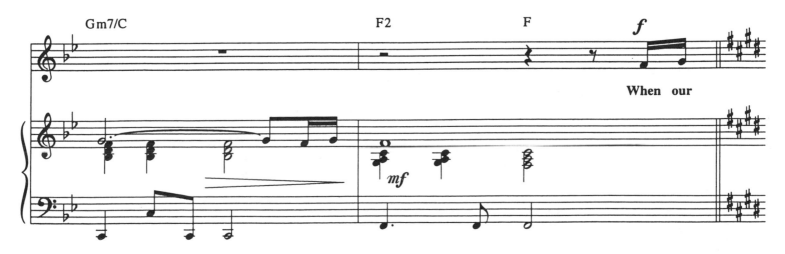

When our

304

eyes are on— the Child— we find all the strength— we need;— all the

strug - gles and— their trials— just turn in - to per - fect peace.—

— We can e - ven start to smile

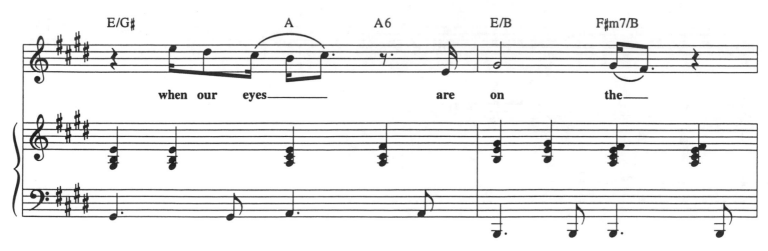

when our eyes———— are on the——

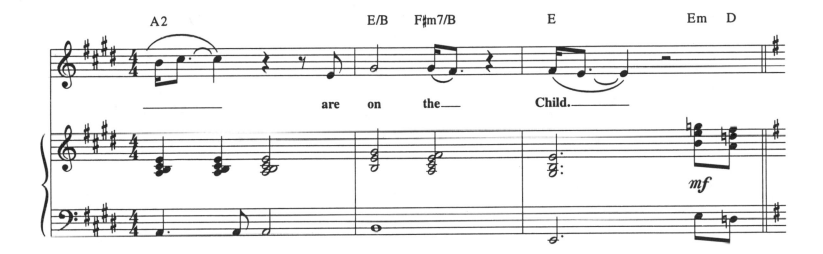

WHEN LOVE CAME DOWN

Written by CHRIS EATON

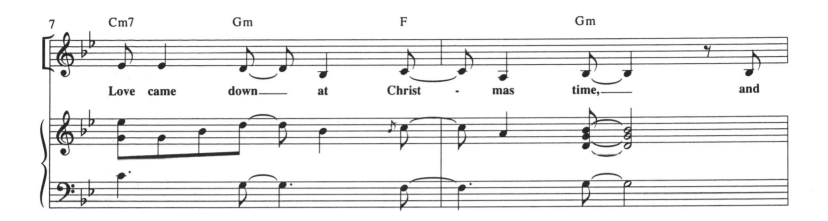

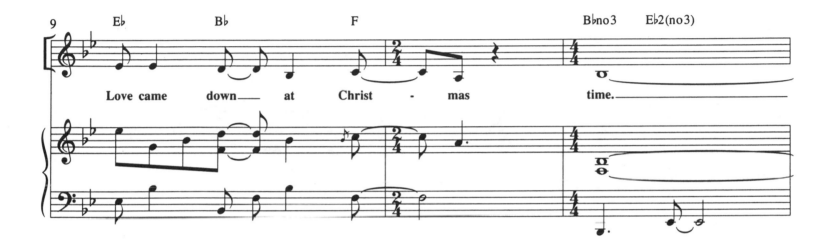

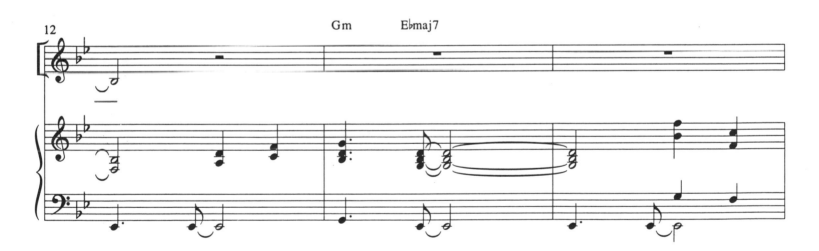

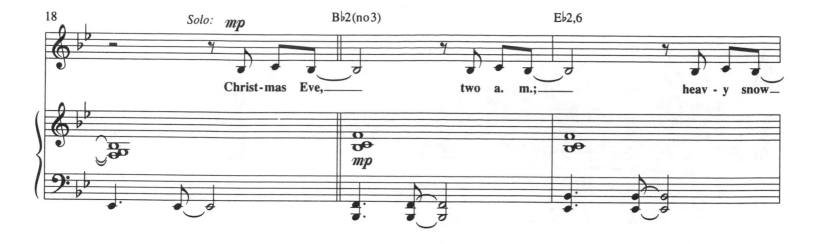

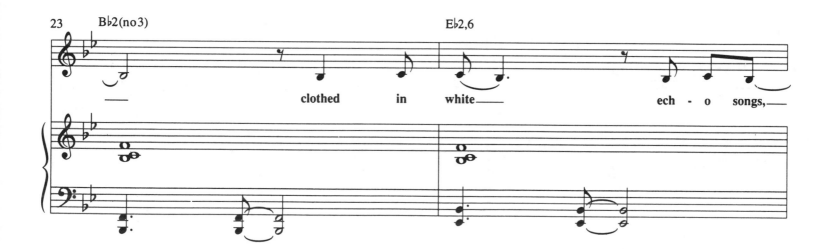

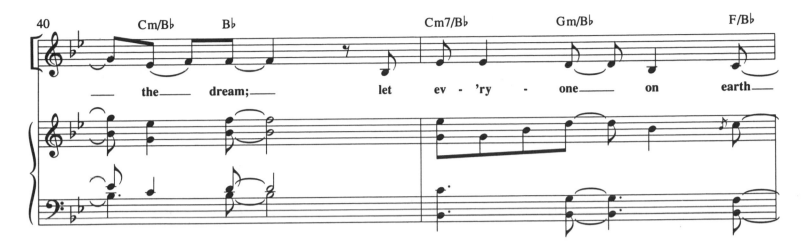

the dream; let ev'ry - one on earth

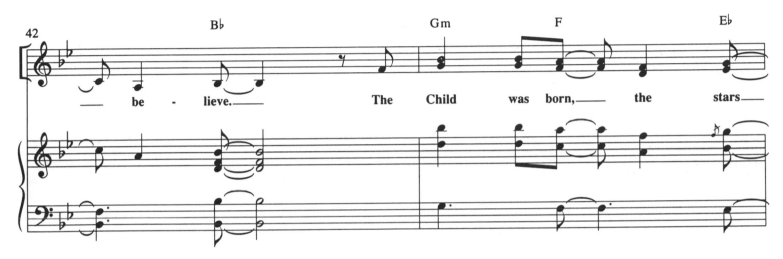

be - lieve. The Child was born, the stars

shone bright, and Love came down at Christ -

- mas time, and Love came down at Christ -

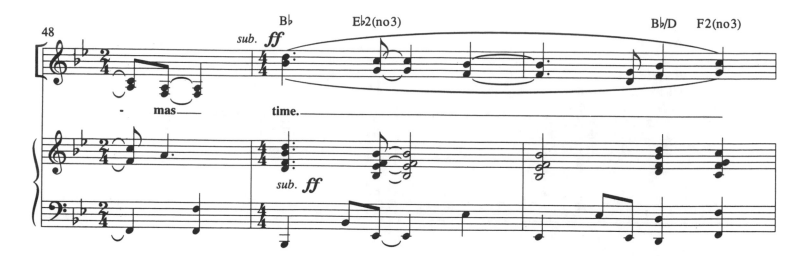

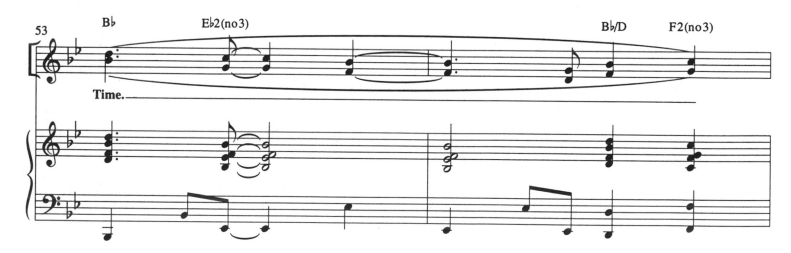

313

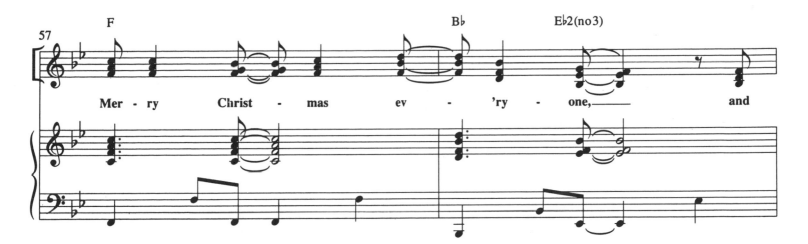

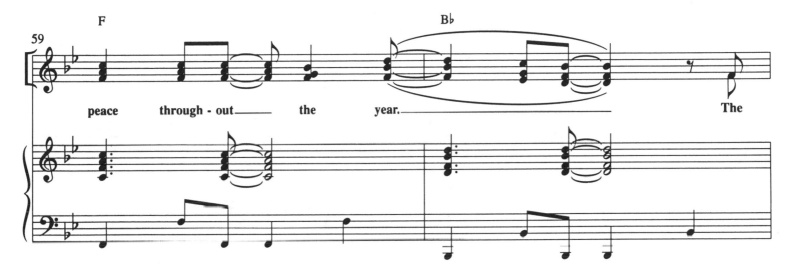

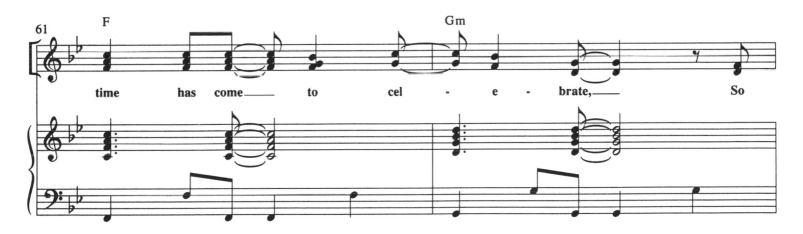

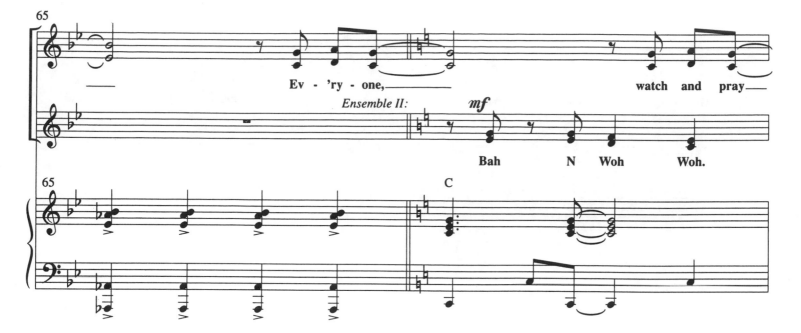

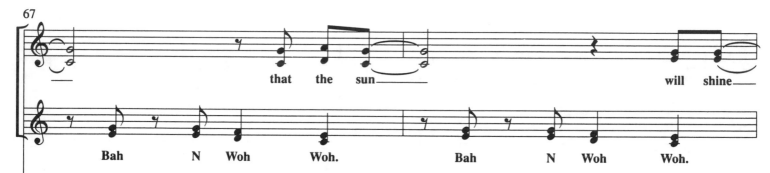

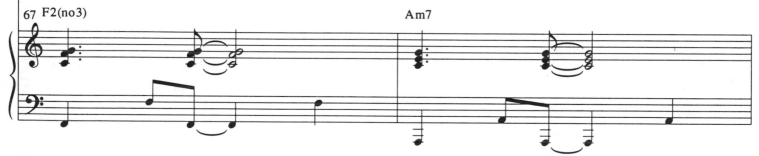

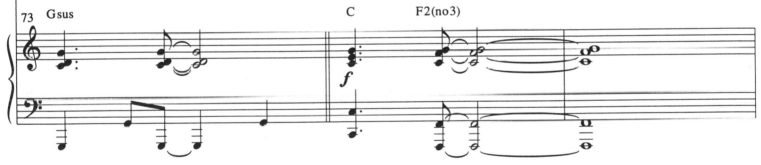

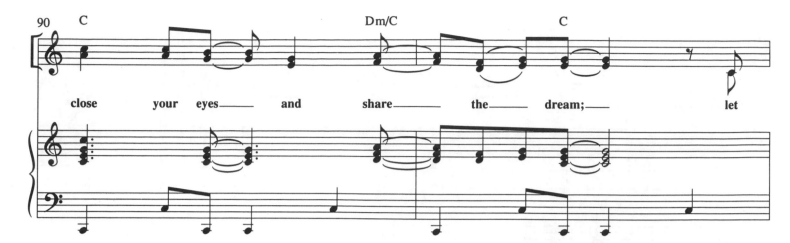

close your eyes____ and share____ the____ dream;____ let

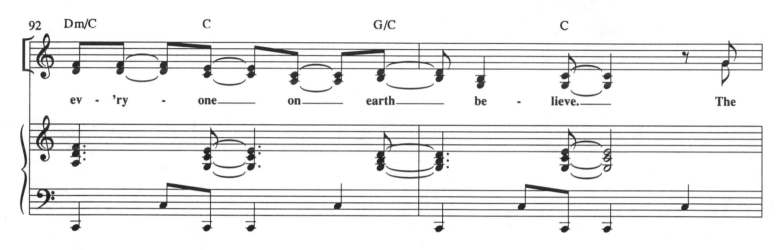

ev - 'ry - one____ on____ earth____ be - lieve.____ The

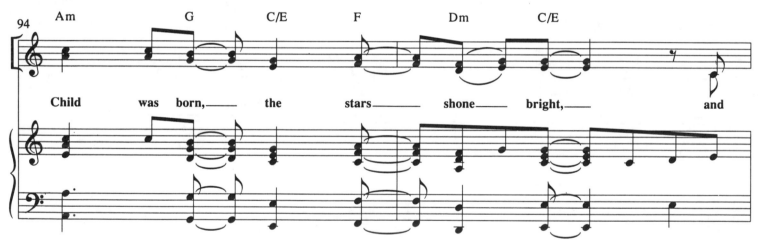

Child was born,____ the stars____ shone____ bright,____ and

Love came____ down____ at____ Christ - mas time.____ Close your eyes____ and share____

the dream;___ let ev - 'ry - one___ on earth___ be - lieve.___ The

Ensemble:

When Love came___

Child was born,___ the stars___ shone___ bright,___ and Love came down___ at Christ -

___ down.___

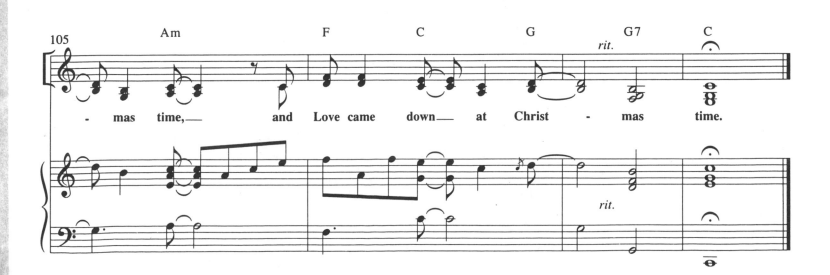

- mas time,___ and Love came down___ at Christ - mas time.

More Contemporary Christian Folios from Hal Leonard

AVALON – A MAZE OF GRACE

This matching folio includes: Adonai • Dreams I Dream for You • Forgive Forget • Knockin' on Heaven's Door • A Maze of Grace • The Move • Reason Enough • Speed of Light • Testify to Love • A World Away.

_____00306239 Piano/Vocal/Guitar $14.95

STEVEN CURTIS CHAPMAN – DECLARATION

13 songs: Bring It On • Carry You to Jesus • Declaration of Dependence • God Follower • God Is God • Jesus Is Life • Live Out Loud • Love Takes You In • Magnificent Obsession • No Greater Love • Savior • See the Glory • This Day • When Love Takes You In.

_____00306453 Piano/Vocal/Guitar $14.95

DC TALK – INTERMISSION: THE GREATEST HITS

17 of dc Talk's best: Between You and Me • Chance • Colored People • Consume Me • Hardway (Remix) • I Wish We'd All Been Ready • In the Light • Jesus Freak • Jesus Is Just Alright • Luv Is a Verb • Mind's Eye • My Will • Say the Words (Now) • Socially Acceptable • SugarCoat It • Supernatural • What If I Stumble.

_____00306414 Piano/Vocal/Guitar $14.95

DELIRIOUS? – SONGS FROM THE CUTTING EDGE

15 songs from this acclaimed 1998 double-disc release: All I Want Is You • Did You Feel the Mountains Tremble? • I Could Sing of Your Love Forever • I'm Not Ashamed • I've Found Jesus • Lord, You Have My Heart • Obsession • more.

_____00306243 Piano/Vocal/Guitar $17.95

JENNIFER KNAPP – LAY IT DOWN

All 10 songs from this 2000 release: All Consuming Fire • Diamond in the Rough • Into You • Lay It Down • A Little More • Peace • Usher Me Down • When Nothing Satisfies • You Answer Me • You Remain. Includes photos.

_____00306358 Piano/Vocal/Guitar $14.95

THE BEST OF SCOTT KRIPPAYNE

Features 10 songs: All My Days • Bright Star Blue Sky • Cross of Christ • Every Single Tear • Hope Has a Way • I Wanna Sing • No More Pretending • Sometimes He Calms the Storm • You Changed the World • You Have Been Good.

_____00306356 Piano/Vocal/Guitar $14.95

THE MARTINS – DREAM BIG

This matching folio includes 10 songs: Come On In • You Come to My Senses • Go Where the Love Flows • Be Strong • Dream Big • We Trust in God • Except for Grace • He'll Be Holdin' His Own • Count Your Blessing • More like a Whisper.

_____00306323 Piano/Vocal/Guitar $14.95

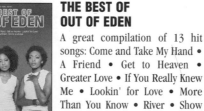

BABBIE MASON – NO BETTER PLACE

10 songs from this gospel diva: Change Me Now • Holy Spirit, You Are Welcome Here • The House That Love Built • I Will Be the One • Isn't That Just like God • Love to the Highest Power • Only God Can Heal • Pray On • Show Some Sign • Stay Up on the Wall.

_____00306357 Piano/Vocal/Guitar $14.95

STACIE ORRICO – GENUINE

This debut release from Orrico features 13 songs: Confidant • Dear Friend • Don't Look at Me • Everything • Genuine • Holdin' On • O.O Baby • Restore My Soul • Ride • So Pray • Stay True • With a Little Faith • Without Love.

_____00306417 Piano/Vocal/Guitar $14.95

THE BEST OF OUT OF EDEN

A great compilation of 13 hit songs: Come and Take My Hand • A Friend • Get to Heaven • Greater Love • If You Really Knew Me • Lookin' for Love • More Than You Know • River • Show Me • There Is a Love • and more.

_____00306381 Piano/Vocal/Guitar $14.95

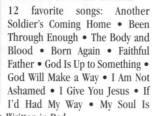

TWILA PARIS – GREATEST HITS

This folio celebrates Twila's career with 18 hits: Destiny • Faithful Friend • God Is in Control • He Is Exalted • How Beautiful • Lamb of God • Sparks and Shadows • The Time Is Now • We Bow Down • We Will Glorify • and more.

_____00306449 Piano/Vocal/Guitar $14.95

JANET PASCHAL – SONGS FOR A LIFETIME

12 favorite songs: Another Soldier's Coming Home • Been Through Enough • The Body and Blood • Born Again • Faithful Father • God Is Up to Something • God Will Make a Way • I Am Not Ashamed • I Give You Jesus • If I'd Had My Way • My Soul Is Anchored to the Rock • Written in Red.

_____00306328 Piano/Vocal/Guitar $14.95

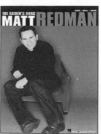

PHILLIPS, CRAIG AND DEAN – LET MY WORDS BE FEW

This 10-song collection includes: Come, Now Is the Time to Worship • How Great You Are • Let Everything That Has Breath • Let My Words Be Few • Open the Eyes of My Heart • You Are My King • Your Grace Still Amazes Me • and more.

_____00306437 Piano/Vocal/Guitar $14.95

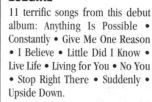

MATT REDMAN – THE FATHER'S SONG

Features 14 songs: The Father's Song • Holy Moment • Justice and Mercy • King of This Heart • Let My Words Be Few • Light of the World • Nothing Is Too Much • O Sacred King • Revelation • Take the World but Give Me Jesus • You Must Increase • more.

_____00306378 Piano/Vocal/Guitar $14.95

REBECCA ST. JAMES – TRANSFORM

Includes 12 songs: All Around Me • Don't Worry • In Me • Intro • For the Love of God • Lean On • My Hope • Reborn • Merciful • One • Stand • Universe • Wait for Me.

_____00306418 Piano/Vocal/Guitar $14.95

ZOEGIRL

11 terrific songs from this debut album: Anything Is Possible • Constantly • Give Me One Reason • I Believe • Little Did I Know • Live Life • Living for You • No You • Stop Right There • Suddenly • Upside Down.

_____00306455 Piano/Vocal/Guitar $14.95